Only an Ap

A Play

Tom Mac Intyre

New Island/New Drama

ONLY AN APPLE
First published 2009
by New Island
2 Brookside
Dundrum Road
Dublin 14
www.newisland.ie

ISBN 978-1-84840-034-4

Printed in Ireland by ColourBooks

New Island received financial assistance from
The Arts Council (An Chomhairle Ealaíon), Dublin, Ireland.

10 9 8 7 6 5 4 3 2 1

ABBEY THEATRE

Amharclann na Mainistreach

Presents

Only an Apple

By Tom Mac Intyre

WORLD PREMIERE

Only an Apple by Tom Mac Intyre was premiered by the Abbey Theatre, at the Peacock, on 21 April 2009.

The Abbey Theatre gratefully acknowledges financial support from The Arts Council/ An Chomhairle Ealaíon

Only An Apple

By Tom Mac Intyre

There will be one interval of 15 minutes

Cast (in alphabetical order)

Sheridan	Malcolm Adams
Elizabeth	Fiona Bell
Grace	Cathy Belton
Mc Phrunty	Steve Blount
The Wife	Tina Kellegher
Hislop	Michael McElhatton
Arkins	Marty Rea
Taoiseach	Don Wycherley

Director	Selina Cartmell
Set Design	Dick Bird
Lighting Design	Matthew Richardson
Choreographer	Ella Clarke
Costume Design	Niamh Lunny
Composer	Conor Linehan
Sound Design	Carl Kennedy
Company Stage Manager	Anne Kyle
Deputy Stage Manager	Amy Burke
Assistant Stage Managers	Bronagh Doherty
	Clare Howe

Voice Director	Andrea Ainsworth
Casting Director	Holly Ní Chiardha (CDG)
Hair and Make-up	Val Sherlock
Photography	Ros Kavanagh
Graphic Design	Red Dog

Please note that the text of the play which appears in this volume may be changed during the rehearsal process and appear in a slightly altered form in performance.

Only An Apple by Tom Mac Intyre is an Abbey Theatre commission

Special thanks to Louis Copeland

Tom Mac Intyre   Writer

Tom Mac Intyre has written many plays for the Abbey Theatre, most notably *The Great Hunger, Sheep's Milk on the Boil, What Happened Bridgie Cleary* and *Good-Evening Mr Collins.* His collaboration with Tom Hickey – most recently in *The Gallant John-Joe* – is of long standing.

CREATIVE TEAM

Selina Cartmell Director

Selina's work at the Abbey Theatre includes *Big Love* by Charles Mee and *Woman and Scarecrow* by Marina Carr. For the Gate Theatre she has directed *Sweeney Todd* (Best Opera Production, Irish Times Theatre Awards), *Festen* and *Catastrophe* as part of the Beckett Centenary Festival (Gate and Barbican, London). Selina is Artistic Director of Siren Productions where work includes *Macbeth, Titus Andronicus* (winner of four Irish Times Theatre Awards including Best Production and Best Director), *La Musica* (Best Production and Best Actress, Dublin Fringe Festival), *Fando & Lis* and *Shutter* (Project Arts Centre). Other productions include *Here Lies* (Galway Arts Festival, Dublin and Paris) and *Passades* (both with Operating Theatre), *Sunlight at Midnight* (BAC, London) and *The Nightingale* (Project Arts Centre). Selina was a finalist in the Opera Europa/Camerata Nouva Europäische Opernregie-Preis (International Directors Opera Award Wiesbaden, Germany 2005). In 2006 she was chosen as a Protégée in the third cycle of the Rolex Mentor and Protégé Arts Initiative, an international philanthropic programme which pairs rising young artists with master artists for a year of mentoring. Selina has just finished collaborating with her mentor, world-renowned director and designer, Julie Taymor. Selina holds an MA (distinction) from Central School of Speech and Drama in Advanced Theatre Practice in Directing and a First Class MA in History of Art and Drama from Trinity College Dublin and Glasgow University. Most recently, Selina directed

Marina Carr's *The Cordelia Dream* for the RSC at
Wilton's Music Hall, London and *The Giant Blue
Hand* by Marina Carr at the Ark, Dublin.

Dick Bird Set Design

Dick last worked at the Abbey Theatre on *Defender of
the Faith*. Other theatre design work includes *La
Grande Magie* (Comedie Francaise), *Lear* (The
Crucible, Sheffield), *El Burlador de Sevilla* (Teatro de
La Abadia), *Swimming With Sharks* (Vaudeville
Theatre, London), *Othello* (Shakespeare's Globe), *The
Enchanted Pig, How Much is Your Iron?, The Three
Musketeers, Monkey!* (Young Vic), *Little Match Girl*
(Tiger Lilies Tour), *Chimps* (Liverpool Everyman and
Playhouse), *Tejas Verdes, Marathon* (Gate), *The Night
Season, The Walls, A Prayer for Owen Meany* (National
Theatre, London), *Harvest, Flesh Wound* (Royal Court),
Rabbit, Heavenly, Dirty Wonderland, Peepshow (for
Frantic Assembly), *True West* (Bristol Old Vic), *The
Wind in the Willows, The Lady in the Van* (West
Yorkshire Playhouse), *The Invisible College* (Salzberg
Festival), *Light* (Théâtre de Complicité), *Closer, My
Fair Lady* (Teatro Nacional, Buenos Aires), *Poseidon,
Icarus Falling* and *Vagabondage* (Primitive Science).
Opera includes *Snegurochka* (Wexford Festival Opera),
Street Scene (Young Vic), *Fidelio, La Cenerentola* (Opera
Theatre Company), *Scenes from the Life of Mozart/Un
Segreto D'Importanza* (Teatro Communale di Bologna
and Teatro dell'Opera di Roma), *The Gondoliers*
(Deutsches Oper Am Rhein), *Il Trittico, The Gambler*
(Opera Zuid, Maastricht), *La Bohème, The Magic Flute*
(LSVO, Vilnius), *Thwaite* (Almeida Opera), *The Rape
of Lucretia* (Guildhall School of Music and Drama),

Die Kunst Des Hungerns (Schauspielhaus, Graz), *Messalina* (Battignano Opera Festival) and *Vollo di Notte, Il Tabarro* (Long Beach Opera). Ballet and dance includes *The Canterville Ghost* (English National Ballet), *Aladdin* (New National Theatre, Tokyo) and *The Banquet* (Protein Dance).

Matthew Richardson   Lighting Design

This is Matthew's first time working at the Abbey Theatre. His lighting designs include *A Midsummer Night's Dream, Hamlet, The Park, The Cordelia Dream* (RSC), *Six Characters Looking for an Author, Doctor Faustus, Hobson's Choice* (Young Vic), *The Birthday Party* and *Nine Plays and a Recipe* (Citizens Theatre, Glasgow). Opera lighting designs include *Otello, Macbeth* (La Scala, Milan), *Eugene Onegin, Lulu* (Glyndebourne), *Fidelio, From The House of the Dead, Pelleas and Melisande* (ENO), *Cherubin, Falstaff* (Royal Opera House), *A Midsummer Night's Dream, Moses and Aron* (Metropolitan Opera, New York), *Don Carlos, Julietta, Peter Grimes* (Paris Opera), *Les Troyens* (Munich Opera), *Jenufa* and *Mefistofele* (Netherlands Opera). Work as a director includes *Macbeth* (Malmö Opera, Sweden), *Rigoletto, Boris Godunov* (New Zealand Opera), *The Cunning Little Vixen, Turandot* (Norrlands Opera, Sweden) and *The Marriage Of Figaro* (BBC Television).

Ella Clarke   Choreographer

Ella's choreographies at the Abbey Theatre include *The Comedy of Errors, Big Love, Romeo and Juliet* and

Woman and Scarecrow. She trained at Rambert School of Dance, London, College of Dance, Dublin and the Perm State Choreographic Institute, Russia, graduating with distinction in 1993. Her work as a performer includes productions for the Abbey Theatre, CoisCéim Dance Theatre, Ciotóg Dance Company, Dance Theatre of Ireland, 2nd Nature (Vienna), Scottish Dance Theatre, Rex Levitates Dance Company and Siren Productions. She has adapted and performed four of eminent experimental choreographer Deborah Hay's solo works. Her choreographies include *Phaedra's Love* (Loose Canon), *The Giant Blue Hand* (The Ark), *Wedding Day at the Cro-Magnons* (Bedrock Productions), *Macbeth, Shutter, Titus Andronicus* (Siren Productions), *Adaptation of a Meeting, Behindtheeyeliesbone* (Myriad Dance Company), *Don Gregorio, Transformations* (Wexford Festival Opera), *Sweeney Todd* and *Anna Karenina* (Gate Theatre). She is co-director of Genesis Project, a practice-based project for radicalisation in the art form of dance. She has been lecturer in dance at DIT Conservatory of Music and Drama since 2002.

Niamh Lunny Costume Design

Niamh is Head of the Costume Department at the Abbey Theatre. Her design work here includes *The Seafarer, Blue/Orange, Homelands, Portia Coughlan* and *I Do Not Like Thee Doctor Fell.* Other work includes *Beware of the Story Book Wolves* (The Ark, nominated for an Irish Times Theatre Award), *Operation Easter* (Calypso), *Here Lies* (Operating Theatre), *Shorts* (Fishamble) and *Rent* (Olympia). She spent four years as costume co-ordinator at the Samuel Beckett Centre where her work included *The Ballad of the Sad Café*, *Dracula*, *Mad Forest*, *The Divorcement of Figaro*, *'Tis Pity She's a Whore*, *Artists and Admirers* and *Stages of the Nation*. Film and television work includes *Studs*, *Dead Bodies*, *Evelyn*, *On Home Ground*, *Anytime Now* and *Black Day at Black Rock*. Niamh is a graduate of Limerick College of Art and Design.

Conor Linehan   Composer

Conor's work at the Abbey Theatre includes scores for *Marble*, *The School for Scandal*, *Homeland*, *The Cherry Orchard*, *The Tempest*, *She Stoops to Conquer*, *The Wake*, *Saint Joan*, *The Colleen Bawn* and *Love in the Title*. Other theatre work includes *The Cordelia Dream*, *The Taming of the Shrew*, *Macbeth*, *Two Gentlemen of Verona*, *Edward the Third*, *Loveplay*, *Luminosity* (RSC), *Peer Gynt*, *The Playboy of the Western World* (National Theatre, London), *American Buffalo*, *A View From the Bridge*, *Long Day's Journey Into Night* (Gate Theatre), *Everyday*, *Dublin by Lamplight* (The Corn Exchange), *The Crock of Gold*, *Antigone* (Storytellers), *Mermaids* (CoisCéim), *Rebecca* (David Pugh Ltd), *Rosencrantz and Guildenstern are Dead*, *Four Knights at Knaresborough* (West Yorkshire Playhouse), *Tartuffe*, *Intemperance*, *The Mollusc*, *The Mayor of Zalamea* (Liverpool Everyman), *Carthaginians*, *A Doll's House* (The Lyric, Belfast) and *Twelfth Night* (Thelma Holt Productions). He has written many scores for radio. In addition he works extensively as a concert pianist and has performed with all of Ireland's major orchestras, premiered concertos by Ronan Guilfoyle and Don Ray as well as performing extensive solo and chamber music repertoire. He wrote a piano concerto for the

RIAM Big Band and Therese Fahy which was premiered at the National Concert Hall and subsequently performed in America and Ireland. He recently toured the United States with the Dublin Philharmonic performing concertos by Beethoven and Shostakovich. Conor is on the piano faculty of the Royal Irish Academy of Music.

Carl Kennedy   Sound Design

Carl's work at the Abbey Theatre includes music and sound design on *The Comedy of Errors* and assistant sound designer on *The Resistible Rise of Arturo Ui*. Other music and sound design work includes *The Giant Blue Hand* with composer Denis Clohessy (The Ark), *Everybody Loves Sylvia* (Randolf SD), *Little Gem* (Gúna Nua), *Phaedra's Love* (Loose Canon), *End of the Line* (Cork Midsummer Festival 2008), *Love's Labour's Lost* (Samuel Beckett Theatre), *Howie the Rookie* (Granary Theatre, Cork), *They Never Froze Walt Disney* (Cork Midsummer Festival 2007 and Dublin Fringe 2008), *A Man in Half* with composer Nico Brown (Theatre Lovett) and *The Shawl* (Bewley's Café Theatre). He was sound designer for *Macbeth* (Siren Productions) and sound co-designer with Denis Clohessy on *Unraveling the Ribbon* (Gúna Nua). Music and sound design for National Youth Theatre includes *At the Black Pig's Dyke*, *The Crucible* (Sligo Youth Theatre), *Beatstreet* (Action Performing in the City in Konstanz, Germany), *Ideal Homes Show*, *Debutantes' Cabaret* (Activate Youth Theatre) and *One Last White Horse*, co-designed with Ian Kehoe (Galway Youth Theatre).

CAST

Malcolm Adams Sheridan

Malcolm's work at the Abbey Theatre includes *The Resistible Rise of Arturo Ui* and *Big Love*. Other theatre credits include Adam in *The Magic Boy* (Yew Tree), The Goat in *The Wonderful World of Dissocia* (Calypso), Grumio in *The Taming of the Shrew* for which he received an Irish Times Theatre Award nomination for Best Supporting Actor, the title role in *Woyzeck* for SEEDS II Showcase (Rough Magic), the title role in *Fr Matthew* (Cork Opera House and tour), *Salomé* (Gate Theatre), *Woyzeck* (Corcadorca), *King Ubu* (Galway Arts Festival), Fr Pat in *Belfry* for which he received an Irish Times Theatre Award nomination for Best Supporting Actor (Livin' Dred), *Mrs Warren's Profession* (Cork Opera House), *Rashomon* (Everyman Palace), *Alice in Wonderland* (Landmark Productions), Charlie Conlon in *Stones in His Pockets* (Duke of Yorks and 40 city UK tour), Tony Ward in *Alone it Stands* (Duchess Theatre, Olympia, Gaiety, Traverse, Edinburgh, the Ten Days on the Island Festival, Tasmania), Young Charlie in *Da* (Irish Repertory Theater, New York), Neville in the American premiere of *Lovechild*, Robert Black in *Public Enemy* (Irish Arts Center), *Under Milk Wood* (Hartford Stage, Connecticut), *The Factory Girls* (Williamstown Theatre Festival, Massachusetts), *King Lear* (Gorilla Rep) and *Dracula* (New York Theater Lab). Films include *Exile in Hell* (Ned Kelly Pictures/TG4) and *Forgiveness* (short) by Jamie O'Neill. He trained in the Actors' Space, New York with Alan Langdon

Fiona Bell   Elizabeth

Fiona's work at the Abbey Theatre includes *Three Sisters, A Month in the Country* and *Medea*. She trained at the Royal Scottish Academy of Music and Drama, Glasgow. Other theatre work includes *Leaves* (Druid, Royal Court), *The Misanthrope* (Chichester Festival), *The Real Thing, See You Next Tuesday, Pride and Prejudice* (Gate Theatre), *How Many Miles to Babylon?* (Second Age), *Dinner with Friends* (Gúna Nua), *Further Than the Furthest Thing, The Country* (Hatch), *Adrenalin Heart* (The Bush), *Animal* (The Red Room), *Richard III, Henry VI, Parts 1, 2 and 3* (RSC and Young Vic), *Snake* (Hampstead Theatre), *Cinderella, Mate in Three, Good, Macbeth, Brilliant Traces,* (Tron Theatre, Glasgow), *Cyrano de Bergerac, Sacred Hearts* (Communicado Theatre, Edinburgh), *Oleanna, Dancing at Lughnasa, Mirandolina, The Masterbuilder, Bedroom Farce* (Royal Lyceum, Edinburgh), *Lament for Arthur Cleary* and *Jump the Life to Come* (7:84, Glasgow). Television credits include *Manhunters, Rockface, Doctors, A Low Winter Sun, The Creatives, Paradise Heights, Eastenders, City Central, Soldier, Soldier, Taggart, Casualty* and *The Bill*. Films include *After Life, Gregory's 2 Girls, Stand and Deliver, Duck, Between Dreams, Nan, I Saw You* and *Trainspotting*. Radio credits include *Sabrina Vasiliev, Poor Things* (*Book at Bedtime*, Radio 4), *Wonderland Girls, Mystery at Ivy Manor* and *50 Friends of Simon Goberschmidt*.

Cathy Belton   Grace

Cathy's work at the Abbey Theatre includes *The Recruiting Officer, The Crucible, The School for Scandal,*

The Playboy of the Western World (tour of Ireland and the US), *The Burial at Thebes, The Plough and the Stars, A Whistle in the Dark, Tartuffe, Medea, The Broken Jug, Living Quarters, A Crucial Week in the Life of a Grocer's Assistant* and *Silverlands*. Other recent theatre work includes *A Solemn Mass for a Full Moon in Summer* (Rough Magic), *The Playboy of the Western World* (Druid, Tokyo Arts Festival), *Uncle Vanya, Festen, A View from the Bridge, Betrayal* (Gate Theatre), *Skylight* (Landmark Productions), *Shiver* (Rough Magic), *Silas Marner, Women in Arms*, for which she was nominated for an Irish Times/ESB Award for Best Actress (Storytellers), *Tine Cnámh, An Trial, Scothsleálta* (Amharclann de hÍde), *True Lines* (Bickerstaffe), *Buddleia, Kitchensink* (The Passion Machine), *The Tempest, Romeo and Juliet, Hamlet* (Island) and *Eclipsed* (Townhall, Galway). Television credits include the lead role of Maura in *Badly Drawn Boy* (BBC series to be screened later this year), *A House in Jerusalem*, Lucy Reilly in *Glenroe, Paths to Freedom* and Kay Corcoran in *Proof*. Films include *Foxes and Savage* (to be released later this year), Sally in John Boorman's *The Tiger's Tail, Intermission*, Paul Mercier's *Before I Sleep* and *Tubberware*. Radio for BBC and RTÉ includes *The Silver Fox, The Power of Darkness, Departures, The Plough and the Stars, The Beebox, Performances, Juno and the Paycock* and *The Irish RM*.

Steve Blount Mc Phrunty

Steve's work at the Abbey Theatre includes *Savoy, Tarry Flynn* (National Theatre, London), *The Wild Duck,*

Judas of the Gallarus, She Stoops to Folly and *The Pauper*. Other theatre credits include *I Swapped My Dad for Two Goldfish* (The Ark), *The Temple of Clown* (Barabbas), *The Night Garden, All My Sons* (Northcott Theatre), *No Place Like Home* (Tinderbox, Belfast), *Romeo and Juliet* (Pavillion), *Oedipus* (Storytellers), *A Whistle in the Dark* (Lyric Theatre, Belfast), *Melody* (Tall Tales), *The Sin Eaters* (New Balance Dance), *Accidental Death of an Anarchist* (Blue Raincoat), *Submarine* (Bewley's Café), *One, Martin Assassin of his Wife* (Pan Pan), *Pilgrims in the Park* (Fishamble), *As You Like It* (Classic Stage) and *Dirty Dusting* (Gaiety, Irish and UK tour). Film and television credits include *The Race, 32A, Single Handed, Prosperity, The Clinic, Stolen Child, Stardust, Breakfast on Pluto, Bachelor's Walk, Fair City, Glenroe, The Colleen Bawn, Agnes Browne, Mad about Mambo, Pips, Johnny Loves Suzy* and *Though the Sky Falls*.

Tina Kellegher   The Wife

Tina's work at the Abbey Theatre includes *The Plough and The Stars, Lovers at Versailles, The Hunt for Red Willie, The Comedy of Errors, The Trojan Women* and *Big Maggie*. Other theatre work includes *A Doll's House* (Lyric Theatre, Belfast), *The Steward of Christendom* (Royal Court Theatre), *Streets of Dublin* (Tivoli Theatre), *Love and a Bottle, Our Country's Good,* (Rough Magic), *Canaries* (Groundwork), *The Madam McAdam Travelling Theatre* (Field Day), *As You Like It* (Second Age), *Little City, Trumpets and Raspberries, The Playboy of the Western World* and *Factory Girls* (Druid Theatre). Film and television credits include *The Clinic, Showbands, Sinners, No Tears, The Snapper,*

Ballykissangel, The Hanging Gale, Murder in Eden and *Scarlett*. Tina recently completed filming on *Happy Ever Afters*. Radio work includes *Baldi* (BBCNI), *The Price of Reputation, Barry Lyndon* (BBC Radio 4) and *Marrying Dad* (RTÉ).

Michael McElhatton Hislop

Michael's work at the Abbey Theatre includes *Romeo and Juliet* and *Twenty Grand*. Other theatre work includes *The Seafarer* (National Theatre, London), *Shining City* (Royal Court/Gate Theatre), *The Wexford Trilogy* (Tricycle), *An Ideal Husband* (Gate Theatre), *The White Devil* (Loose Canon), *Car Show* (The Corn Exchange), *Greatest Hits, The Midnight Court* (Project Arts Centre), *The Way of the World* (Rough Magic), *A Decision Pure and Simple* (Riverside Studio), *An Enemy of the People* (Young Vic), *As You Like It* (Rose Theatre), *The Wind in the Willows* (Sheffield Crucible), *Little Malcolm and the Struggle Against the Eunuchs* (BAC), *Handsome, Handicapped and Hebrew* (Grove Theatre), *Elizabeth Barton* (Tabard Theatre) and *Water Music* (Cockpit Theatre). Films include *Perrier's Bounty, Fifty Dead Men Walking, Happy Ever Afters, The Tiger's Tail, Mickyboy and Me, Spin the Bottle, Intermission, The Actors, Blowdry, Saltwater, Crush Proof, Just in Time, All Souls' Day, I Went Down* and *November Afternoon*. Television credits include *Father and Son, Single Handed III, Whistleblower, Hide and Seek, Paths to Freedom,* for which he received an Irish Film and Television Award for Best Actor, *Fergus's Wedding,* (RTÉ), *Aristocrats, Vicious Circle, Rebel Heart, The Ambassador* (BBC) and *My Boy Jack*.

Writing credits include *Paths to Freedom, Fergus's Wedding* and *Spin the Bottle*.

Marty Rea Arkins

Marty's work at the Abbey Theatre includes *An Ideal Husband, Saved, The Big House* and Cecily Cardew in *The Importance of Being Earnest*. Other theatre credits include *Improbable Frequency* (Rough Magic New York tour), *Philadelphia, Here I Come!* (Second Age), *The Glass Menagerie, Salomé* (Gate Theatre), *The Parker Project* (Rough Magic), *Jack and the Beanstalk* (Waterfront Hall), *Smilin' Through* (Truant Theatre), *The Session* (Dubbeljoint), *Henry IV* (RADA Enterprises), *Philadelphia, Here I Come!* (Art NI), *Married Bliss* and *Bell, Book and Candle* (Centre Stage). Film and television credits include *Vingt Minutes*. Radio includes *Marrying Dad* (RTÉ), *Getting Away from It, One Day in the Life of Ivan Denisovich, Swan Song* (Radio 4), *Under the Hawthorn Tree* and *Adam's Starling* (BBC NI). Marty graduated from RADA in 2002.

Don Wycherley Taoiseach

Most of Don's theatre work has been at the Abbey Theatre including *The Seafarer, Fool for Love, A Month in the Country, The Shaughraun, Eden, A Whistle in the Dark, The House, Translations, The Last Apache Reunion, The Honeyspike, Tarry Flynn, The Muesli Belt, Portia Coughlan* and *The Comedy of Errors*, to mention but a few. Other theatre work includes *The Giant Blue Hand* (The Ark), *Conversations on a Homecoming*

(Livin' Dred) and *Poor Beast in the Rain* (Gate Theatre). Television credits include *The Running Mate, Showbands, Bachelor's Walk, Ballykissangel, Black Day at Black Rock, Father Ted, Filleann an Feall* and *Making the Cut*. Films include *Ondine, Wide Open Spaces, Speed-Dating, Garage, Shrooms, Veronica Guerin, When Brendan Met Trudy, Sweeney Todd, The Last of the High Kings, Michael Collins, I Went Down, One Man's Hero* and *The General*.

ABBEY THEATRE
Amharclann na Mainistreach

NEXT AT THE ABBEY

THE LAST DAYS OF A RELUCTANT TYRANT
By Tom Murphy
Directed by Conall Morrison
27 May –11 July
AT THE ABBEY
WORLD PREMIERE

THE RIVALS
By Richard Brinsley Sheridan
Directed by Patrick Mason
22 July –19 September
AT THE ABBEY

Booking Áirithintí
00 353 1 87 87 222
www.abbeytheatre.ie

Fáilte go hAmharclann na Mainistreach, amharclann náisiúnta na hÉireann

Osclaíodh doirse Amharclann na Mainistreach ar Shráid na Mainistreach ar an 27 Mí na Nollag 1904, le W. B. Yeats agus Bean Augusta Gregory mar stiúrthóirí. Ba iad a réamhtheachtaithe ná Amharclann Liteartha na hÉireann agus Cumann Drámata Náisiúnta Frank agus Willie Fay. Ar an 31 Mí Eanáir 2006 rinneadh an chuideachta seo a dhíscaoileadh agus bunaíodh cuideachta nua, Abbey Theatre Amharclann Na Mainistreach, a reáchtálann an amharclann anois. Níor tháinig aon athrú ar bheartas ealaíne Amharclann na Mainistreach go fóill agus cuimsíonn sé na spriocanna seo a leanas:

- Chun infheistíocht a dhéanamh i scríbhneoirí agus in ealaíontóirí nua Éireannacha mar aon le hiad a chur chun cinn

- Chun clár bliantúil de drámaíocht Éireannach agus idirnásiúnta a sholáthar atá éagsúil, tarraingteach agus nuálach.

- Chun réimse leathan custaiméirí a mhealladh is a ghníomhú agus chun eispéiris spreagúla, a thugann orthu teacht ar ais, a sholáthar

- Chun timpeallacht oibre bhríomhar a chruthú a sholáthraíonn cleachtas scothdomhanda ar ud ár ngnó

I 1925, thug Saorstát nua na hÉireann fóirdheontas bliantúil neamhghnách d'Amharclann na Mainistreach, agus tháinig sí ina céad amharclann fóirdheonaithe stáit i dtíortha an Bhéarla. Coinníonn ar An Chomhairle Ealaíon, mar aon lenár gcuid cairde ár bpatrúin agus sibhse, ár lucht féachana, tacaíocht a thabhairt dár gcuid oibre.

I 1951, rinneadh damáiste do bhunfhoirgnimh Amharclann na Mainistreach de bharr dóiteáin. Athlonnaíodh Amharclann na Mainistreach go dtí Amharclann na Banríona. Cuig bliana déag cothrom an lae sin anonn, ar an 18 Iúil 1966, bhog Amharclann na Mainistreach foirgneamh nua, a dhear Michael Scott, ar an láthair chéanna.

I Meán Fómhair 2006 d'fhógair an Rialtas go mbeadh comórtas dearaidh idirnáisiúnta ar siúl chun ionad buan nua a chruthú d'Amharclann na Mainistreach, a bheidh suite ar Ché Sheoirse i mBaile Átha Cliath. I nDeireadh Fómhair 2007 fógraíodh an coiste moltóireachta don chomórtas.

Idir an dá linn, thugamar faoi chlár athchóirithe agus uasghrádaithe d'fhonn cur leis an eispéire as dár gcuid ealaíontóirí agus daoibhse, a lucht féachana. Chuimsigh sé seo an t-athchumrú radacach, ar cuireadh fáilte fhorleathan roimhe, in halla éisteachta Amharclann na Mainistreach.

Go raibh maith agaibh as bheith linn don léiriú seo. Tá súil againn go mbainfidh sibh taitneamh as an seó agus tá súil againn nach fada eile arís go mbeidh sibh inár gcuideachta in Amharclann na Mainistreach.

Welcome to the Abbey Theatre, Ireland's national theatre

The Abbey Theatre opened its doors on Abbey Street on 27 December 1904, with W. B. Yeats and Lady Augusta Gregory as its directors. Its precursors were the Irish Literary Theatre and Frank and Willie Fay's National Dramatic Society. The company originally traded as the National Theatre Society Limited. On 31st January 2006 this company was dissolved and a new company established, Abbey Theatre Amharclann Na Mainistreach, which now runs the theatre. The artistic policy of the Abbey remains unchanged and incorporates the following ambitions:

- Invest in and promote new Irish writers and artists
- Produce an annual programme of diverse, engaging, innovative Irish and international theatre
- Attract and engage a broad range of customers and provide compelling experiences that inspire them to return
- Create a dynamic working environment which delivers world best practice across our business

In 1925, the Abbey Theatre was given an annual subsidy by the new Free State, becoming the first ever state-subsidised theatre in the English speaking world. The Arts Council of Ireland/An Chomhairle Ealaíon, along with our friends, patrons, benefactors and you, our audience, continues to support our work.

In 1951, the original buildings of the Abbey Theatre were damaged by fire. The Abbey re-located to the Queen's Theatre. Fifteen years to the day later, on 18 July 1966, the Abbey moved back to its current home, designed by Michael Scott, on the same site.

In September 2006 the Government announced that an international design competition would be held to create a new home for the Abbey, to be located at George's Dock in Dublin. In October 2007 the jury for the competition was announced.

In the meantime, we have undertaken a programme of refurbishment and upgrade to enhance the experience for our artists and for you, the audience. This included the radical and widely welcomed reconfiguration of the Abbey auditorium.

Thank you for joining us for this production. We hope you enjoy the show and look forward to welcoming you again soon to the Abbey.

Board
Bryan McMahon (Chairman), Catherine Byrne, Tom Hickey, Olwen Fouéré, John Finnegan Suzanne Kelly, Declan Kiberd, Dr Jim Mountjoy, Eugene O'Brien, Maurice O'Connell, Lynne Parker

Executive
Fiach Mac Conghail	Director
Declan Cantwell	Director of Finance and Administration
Oonagh Desire	Director of Development
Aideen Howard	Literary Director
Sally Anne Tye	Director of Public Affairs
Tony Wakefield	Director of Technical Services and Operations

Only an Apple

Characters

Taoiseach
Elizabeth I A beautiful redhead, English, young …
Grace O'Malley Beautiful, dark-haired, Irish, óg …

(Elizabeth wears a tasteful crown, and lots of jewellery.
That said, her dress is queenly, blends the modern and
the 16th century. Grace is in piratical mode; her
ensemble, à la Elizabeth's, is period but would not be
out of place at last night's rock concert.)

Sheridan A butler
Hislop Press Secretary
Arkins Cultural Attaché
The wife …
Mc Phrunty The overweight Taoiseach-in-waiting

ACT ONE
SCENE ONE

Opulent living-room of the **Taoiseach***'s country residence,*
Taraford. Sunlight through the great French window,
centrally placed, which dominates the upstage zone. The
room has a flurry of doors. Photos and paintings (huge),
consistently garish, dominate the walls. They present the
Taoiseach *skiing, surfing, golfing, and so on.* **Taoiseach**
in silk pyjamas, ornate dressing-gown, fulsome slippers,
improbable cravat. **Taoiseach** *to the phone, dials. We're*
permitted to hear called as well as caller.

Hislop Hello?

Taoiseach How is my tireless press secretary this
morning?

Hislop Alert, Taoiseach, alert.

Taoiseach Very good, Hislop. Now. This banal
business of the heave. Mc Phrunty has to be shafted.
With no delay. See you here in half an hour.

Hislop Done, Taoiseach.

Taoiseach Oh – and bring Arkins.

Hislop *He*'ll be a great help.

Taoiseach Cultural attachés are not paid to help. *Tone*
is their shtick.

Phone down.

Taoiseach (*to audience*) Mc Phrunty – The Inflated-in-Waiting! Few things excite me more than a heave. I was born some night of the long knives!

Taoiseach *strolls upstage, flings open the window. Wolfhounds begin to howl melodiously.* **Taoiseach** *dons white gloves, removes lid from a convenient bin, flings a succession of bloodied bones to the hounds. Tumult subsides, gloves discarded. Enter* **Sheridan** *with morning papers and breakfast.*

Sheridan (*broad Cavan accent*) Good mornin', Taoiseach.

Taoiseach Black coffee only, Sheridan.

Sheridan Taoiseach?

Taoiseach Black coffee only.

Sheridan The juice, Taoiseach? The stirabout?

Taoiseach Black coffee, please.

Sheridan No bother, Taoiseach, no bother.

Coffee poured.

Taoiseach Thank you. Morning papers singing the same old song?

Sheridan Right, Taoiseach. Claimin' he has the numbers.

Taoiseach Shredder.

2

Sheridan No bother, Taoiseach.

Sheridan *to the shredder with the dailies, feeds the dailies
to it. Vengeful hum of the shredder rouses the wolfhounds.
They want more, more, more …* **Sheridan** *moves to
placate them, goes to the bin (no need of gloves), gets the
goodies, hurls them to the hounds. Happy sounds of the
pack gobbling.*

Taoiseach The bastards have just *been* fed – why do I
keep them? For the din?

Sheridan (*wiping his hands on a stray newspaper page*)
They're not the worst, Taoiseach, the bit o' company
when people's a burden.

Taoiseach *strolls, preoccupied.* **Sheridan** *waits.*

Taoiseach Sheridan?

Sheridan Taoiseach?

Taoiseach How, in your view, will I break Pretender
Mc Phrunty's back?

Sheridan Give him rope, Taoiseach.

Taoiseach Yes?

Sheridan Shure doesn't the world know he's a patent-
leather eegyut?

Taoiseach Sheridan, know something? We may, and
not for the first time, be thinking along largely the
same lines!

Sheridan Rope's cheap, Taoiseach, I always heard.
And handy for hangin'.

Taoiseach Precisely. Now, listen to me. I have a wife.

Sheridan She's well, Taoiseach?

Taoiseach Flu on the mend. I have a charming
companion.

Sheridan She's well, Taoiseach?

Taoiseach Still in the huff. But the breaking news is
two other women have entered my life. And my hunch
is they may very well spell Mc Phrunty's demise. With
a little encouragement from me. Naturally.

Sheridan *gobsmacked.*

Taoiseach Say something, for God's sake. Say 'Sorry
for your trouble' or 'Congratulations' or 'Who won the
Derby?' – but, Godammit, say something!

Sheridan They're comin' to visit, Taoiseach?

Taoiseach They're here! I discovered them this
morning. Looking out a window.

Sheridan Lukin outa win–

Taoiseach What has compelled them? No idea.
Correction, I feel they've been *sent*. There's an
instrumental something about them. And therefore I
say, *Woe betide, Mc Phrunty*. Other times, I confess,
I've no idea what their game is, no idea, none!

Sheridan   Did ye think of askin' the ladies, Taoiseach?

Taoiseach   Sheridan?

Sheridan   Taoiseach?

Taoiseach   Will you go now to the Mauve Room of the West Wing and bring here my two guests?

Sheridan   No bother, Taoiseach, no bother.

Sheridan *exiting.*

Taoiseach   What time is it?

Sheridan   Half-nine, Taoiseach.

Exit **Sheridan**.

Taoiseach   (*to audience*) Someone said to me once – young deputy up from the bogs – first term in the house – 'You never wear a watch, Taoiseach?' 'No,' I told him, 'I never was. But I've known lots who *were* and battalions who *are*. All they do is *tick,* and when they're not ticking they're alarming, when they're not alarming they're bloodless gadgets falling to bits at forty – and then *insisting* on a State Funeral!' Young deputy's eyes now one-arm-banditing in their sockets – he was mine for life. Kill for me. Detail. Everything's in the detail.

Taoiseach *casually does the rounds of the pictures, adjusting (many are hanging visibly awry), flicking dust away, removing an invisible smudge from a frame. In the middle of doing this, he halts, goes happily pensive, has news for the audience.*

Taoiseach They belong – my guests – they belong, in a sense, to an earlier age, some golden age, and yet they're of the *now* – so contemporary – contemporary as do-it-yourself-in-manacles!

Taoiseach *to the window, the sunlight, euphoria …*

ACT ONE
SCENE TWO

Elizabeth *and* **Grace** *come quietly into the room,*
Taoiseach *unaware. The two settle into playing cards,*
with intense concentration. (Lute notes, gentle?) The
Taoiseach *eventually senses their presence, turns, takes*
them in, comes downstage.

Taoiseach (*to audience*) We have our quirks – and
why not? Never knew anyone of moment who wasn't a
snake-pit of compulsions.

The two remain wrapped up in the card game. **Taoiseach**
tours the space, happily, watching his guests, considering
options, decides. Advances, confiscates every card in sight,
and pockets the haul. The women, at once, rise.
Normality, it seems, has been restored.

Taoiseach I understand fever – it follows us around.

Elizabeth He understands –

Grace Doesn't have to be understood!

Elizabeth *embraces the* **Taoiseach**, *full-blooded kiss, tosses*
him in **Grace***'s direction.* **Grace** *grips him.*

Grace Show me your teeth. I love cold teeth in a
man!

Elizabeth May I have a drink?

Grace Bare them!

Knock, and enter **Sheridan**, *curious to say the least.*

Taoiseach Sheridan – Elizabeth the First and Ms Grace O'Malley.

Sheridan (*in a whirl*) Majesty … Ms O'Malley …

Polite nods from the women for the servant class.

Grace Your teeth, Taoiseach!

Elizabeth I thought the Irish drank non-stop.

Taoiseach *yields to* **Grace***'s request.* **Grace** *raps the teeth with a ring she's wearing (mike the sound).* **Sheridan** *is hard put not to intervene.*

Grace The real ally-dally, Taoiseach! Doubt ye bhoy!

Taoiseach Thank you, Sheridan.

Sheridan Would ye rather me to stay, Taoiseach?

Taoiseach I said – is your hearing suddenly impaired? – I said 'Thank you, Sheridan.'

Sheridan (*exiting*) I'll be in the vexicinity if ye want me, Taoiseach.

Taoiseach (*snarl*) Noted.

Sheridan *gone.*

Elizabeth For positively the last time, a drink would be a help.

Taoiseach Forgive me, Majesty ... Jameson, Scotch, Bourbon? Something lighter? We have some superb white wines.

Elizabeth Red wine for sleep –

Grace White wine for play –

Elizabeth White let it be!

Taoiseach And you, Grace?

Grace JJ & S, like a dacent man.

Taoiseach *Smahán* of the hard stuff!

The **Taoiseach**, *lick of hysteria, fixes the drinks, humming* 'I Dreamt that I Dwelt in Marble Halls'. *He presents the drinks.*

Taoiseach Majesty – Grace – your very good healths.

Grace Takin' nothin' yerself, man?

Taoiseach Black coffee pro tem, Grace.

Elizabeth He's feeling his way!

Taoiseach Never alcohol before noon, Majesty.

Elizabeth You're lying – but I revere liars.

Grace Taoiseach, there was this go-boy, Bingham, dwarf somewhere in the genes, stallion in the eye, we're talkin' the fifteen—

Taoiseach Eighties, yes, heard of him.

Elizabeth Pint-Pot Bingham!

Grace Sir Pint-Pot. I was the mortal enemy, pursued by land and sea. Only a slip of a lassie but I knew what he was *really* after. Captured me, had a grand new gallows built for my execution, and in the shadow of that gallows, men are so –

Elizabeth Gothic?

Grace (*nod of assent*) He took me till he was empty. Then lets me go. Week later he's dead, God rest him. I've been thinking, Taoiseach, isn't it time for a memorial to mark that sweaty Gael-an'-Gall night in Galway, could you –

Taoiseach Consider it done. Connemara marble?

Grace Mighty number! Thanks, Taoiseach, I know you're a busy man.

Taoiseach More than busy – I've a heave on my lap – Fireside Chat to the nation – State Visit to Japan – and The Minister of Finance is a deliquescent alcoholic!

Elizabeth Is that piano tuned?

Taoiseach I believe so, Majesty. Seldom used but –

Elizabeth, *airing her beautiful hands, to the piano. She sits, gives us a blast of 'Greensleeves'.*

Grace She just wants us to admire her hands, Taoiseach.

Taoiseach They are, Majesty, beautiful hands.

Elizabeth (*leaving the piano*) Teeshuck, I'm not a great one for memorials. I am, dare I say, my own memorial. The fashioning of that, I can tell you, was no small task, yet I had sustenance.

Grace Why wouldn't ye!

Elizabeth I have never been able to breathe without the intimacy of powerful, adoring men. That, Twosocks, is why we're here. Your fame, your storied boudoir prowess, your style – 'Lick the hand if you can't lop it' – did you really say that to the pope?

Taoiseach The things people invent!

Grace Dead duck in the post to impident opponents!

Taoiseach Nothing flies like a good story!

Elizabeth And a surveillance system that would make my much-vaunted Secret Service look like a slow waltz with a wooden leg. What are you thinking of, Twosack?

Grace Us!

Taoiseach Nothing.

Grace An' what do ye think of when yer thinkin' o' nothin'?

Taoiseach Women's broken promises! And what's this thing you have about teeth?

11

Elizabeth Good, Threesock, press her, press her hard!

Grace I'm a *teeth* person – I'm a pirate, amn't I?
Shouldn't boast, but men, to a man, learn to *crave* my
incisors.

Taoiseach Your preferences, Majesty?

Elizabeth My preferences, Tassock, rest in my hands.
I love to play the keyboard of *l'amour*, listen to the
music, let appetites moisten, then let myself the
keyboard be!

Taoiseach You're an artist!

Elizabeth And you know what that means, Trussock?

Taoiseach Tell me ...

Elizabeth I never know when to stop! Keyboard
Elizabeth must encourage pliant pianist towards
trembling chords and steep arpeggios to melt the cares
of office and the calendar beguile!

Taoiseach – *of a sudden – unresponsive, gloomy, in a
state.*

Grace We frighten him, Bess.

Elizabeth Do we, Truelock, do we?

Taoiseach No, no, not at all – I assure you.

Grace Not going to cut bait an' run, are you now?

Elizabeth We've been too –

Taoiseach No, no, I'm merely cogitating.

Grace He's 'cogitating'!

Elizabeth Men in Great Place must cogitate. Very well! Let them cogitate!

The **Taoiseach** *paces, morose.*

Elizabeth *and* **Grace** *to the window. The wolfhounds go into a (well-nigh) worshipful chorale. The two wave, take a bow. Chorale continues.* **Elizabeth** *steadies herself, with a savage arm-gesture ordains silence, and the two turn back to the pacing* **Taoiseach.** *He halts, comes towards them.*

Taoiseach Look. The position is this …

The two instantly go into peals of laughter – they can't stop. They find seats, eventually control themselves. **Taoiseach** *is viewing them with a certain impatience and unease.*

Grace It's the way it came out of you, *a chroí* …

Elizabeth It's what men always say, Toolsack – don't mind us.

Grace 'Look, the position is this' – me ould fella's last croak!

Diversion: **Elizabeth** *focuses on a door to the left, say. The door in question swings open obediently,* **Elizabeth** *rises, and, without yea or nay, sweeps through that open door and vanishes.* **Taoiseach,** *thrown, hastens after her. Another door whips open and* **Grace,** *modestly pensive,* *strolls through it. The door closes behind her.* **Taoiseach** *back in the space, in something of a spin.*

Taoiseach   Good God! Sheridan – SHERIDAN –

He presses a button, urgent buzzer sound, enter **Sheridan**.

Sheridan   Taoiseach?

Taoiseach   Where are my guests?

Sheridan   Guests, Taoiseach?

Taoiseach   'Guests, Taoiseach' – you did meet my guests?

Sheridan   Oh – the ladies – yes, Taoiseach.

Taoiseach   So the memory's not completely shattered?

Sheridan   Divil the bit, Taoiseach. I can see them parked there, plain as porpentine.

Taoiseach   You recall their names, perhaps?

Sheridan   Queen Elizabeth the First and Ms Grace O'Malley, Taoiseach.

Taoiseach   They've vanished!

Sheridan   No bother, Taoiseach.

Taoiseach   What do you mean – 'No bother'?

Sheridan   All I meant was, Taoiseach, well, women – they'll vanish. Turn yer back – they're gone!

Taoiseach   Fuck the pair of them – scented cobwebs!

Sheridan   Lots says, Taoiseach, they're not worth the bother –

Taoiseach   *Manana* punani!

Sheridan   For the ree-raws they combusht. An' them hardly tryin'!

Taoiseach   Pixillated cunts! Black coffee, please.

Coffee supplied.

Sheridan   Sup o' the craythur in it, Taoiseach?

Taoiseach *sits, drinks the coffee as if it were poison.*

Taoiseach   Women. What is it? They appear. Alter everything. They vanish.

Sheridan   That's my larnin' process with them, Taoiseach, not makin' meself out to have a whisker of a sniff of what they do be up to.

Taoiseach   Why do they vanish?

Sheridan   They can't help it, Taoiseach. Just the cut o' them.

Taoiseach   (*steadying*) Maybe it's a good that they vanish?

Sheridan *treats himself to a succulent chuckle.*

Sheridan   Yer not the first came out with that verdick, Taoiseach.

Taoiseach Perhaps I imagined the pair o' them?

Sheridan That happens too, Taoiseach, oftener nor you'd think.

Screeching of the peacocks on the lawn intrudes.

Taoiseach Bloody peacocks – 'Birds of Venus' my royal Irish arse!

Sheridan *hurries to it, a bucket handy, food hurled, din of peacock feeding-frenzy.*

Taoiseach How many doors has this room, Sheridan?

Sheridan One, two, three, four, Taoiseach.

Taoiseach It was like all the doors opened and shut at once – and they're gone!

Sheridan I'll take a dander around the place, Taoiseach, see if I –

Crazed chorus of the peacocks again.

Taoiseach Put the wolfhounds on those stilted castrati.

Sheridan *to the window. Whistle signal. The hounds arrive. Howling peacocks, screaming, take flight. Silence.*

Taoiseach Thank you, Sheridan.

Sheridan To be sure, Taoiseach. In the vicinity, ekskettera, ekskettera.

Exit **Sheridan.**

Taoiseach *sits, sips coffee, puts coffee aside, strolls downstage.*

Taoiseach Sometimes I wish I were a watch, I genuinely do. It would make things so simple, so digitally simple. I believe I could get to like it. Vasectomy of the soul! (*He brightens*) There's an elegant phrase (*he jots it in a notebook*). I must try it out on Cherie – when she gets over the huff. '*Ma belle,* the hot news is I'm lined up for a soul-vasectomy, Tuesday week, three-thirty.' 'You're lined up for *what?*'(*Long pause, he goes pensive again*) That pair haven't left, they're around, they know what they want, and they get what they want, that's what I love about them, minges *growling* for it, the *honesty* of it is – captivating!

He settles, sips his coffee, everything to play for.

ACT ONE
SCENE THREE

Rap on the door, enter **Hislop** *and* **Arkins**.

Hislop See the morning papers, Taoiseach?

Taoiseach Hislop is harassed.

Arkins They're swearing that ignoramus has the numbers!

Taoiseach Arkins is anxious.

Hislop Meeting of the Parliamentary Party tonight, Taoiseach. Don't we strike first?

Taoiseach Hislop is *hunted*.

Arkins Are the press in that infant's *pay*?

Taoiseach Arkins is *addled*.

Hislop Taoiseach, *have you studied the morning rags?*

For answer, **Taoiseach** *dances, giddy, to the shredder. Showers himself with ribbons of paper, romps about the space festooned with the offending newsprint.*

Taoiseach I'm in *the news*! And I adore *being in the news*! Please –

He halts, waits for the pair to attend, carefully free him from the web of newsprint.

18

Taoiseach Thank you. Now. Truth of the matter – I feel so good after that – should I go on the stage? – truth of the matter is I'm in the news for a reason, reasons, *un*reasons galore, all, my good friends, quite outside your ken.

Hislop You've shafted Mc Phrunty?

Arkins A night-strike?

Taoiseach You do mistake my meaning, friends! The heave is on the margin. There are, I repeat, events *en train*, before which you, the media, the world at large, will stand amazed!

Hislop The Party have turned on that thick – he's toast?

Arkins The White House – address to Senate and Congress?

Hislop Beijing – Special Trade Pact?

Taoiseach Let me not keep you in suspense. We have here in Taraford –

A door opens of its own accord. Enter **Elizabeth** *and* **Grace***, talking quietly, simply (it appears) passing through. The three males gape. Just as the two are exiting, another door opening to their imperious advance, the* **Taoiseach** *comes to life.*

Taoiseach Majesty? Grace? (*The two turn*) Queen Elizabeth the First and Ms Grace O'Malley – Press Secretary Hislop and our Cultural Attaché, The Poet Arkins.

The women nod urbanely towards the named and shaken males, who respond in disheveled fashion: Great pleasure, ma'am … Glad to meet you, Ms O'Malley … *and the women continue on their way.*

Taoiseach   Not staying, Ladies?

Elizabeth   *Plus tard,* Tussock, *plus tard.*

Taoiseach   A pleasure delayed, Majesty!

The women exit.

Taoiseach   Aren't they extraordinary? They're here to offer – discovery? Delight? The turbulent landscape of the new? Certainly, I feel a fated something in their arrival.

Hislop   When – arrival – where the –

Taoiseach   This morning – I met them on a corridor. The heave? Diminishes, doesn't it, on the instant? What price Mc Phrunty as cunt-fodder for the pair! Beyond that, I scarcely dare speculate – but we're certainly talking a new ball-game, new playing-field, new rules, vistas undreamt of – what a century we inhabit, Gentlemen! Any thoughts, Hislop? Sing for your supper!

Hislop *walks grimly downstage, stares into the mist.*

Taoiseach   Hislop is *distrait*! '*Amlet ou Le Distrait!*'

Hislop *comes to.*

Hislop   Taoiseach, you have a wonderful wife.

Taoiseach Flu victim.

Hislop You have a charming and beautiful companion.

Taoiseach Wrapped in a huff.

Hislop And you've a heave on your lap.

Taoiseach Which always brings out the best in me.

Hislop Do you really need two brazen free-loaders prancing the premises, the pair – no question of it – sent here by Mc Phrunty's crew, their fingerprints all over it, Taoiseach caught with his pants down, suspenders flyin', you're out, he's in, country hurled into shambles. Get them outa there. If the affair leaks – and it will – we fast-forward into spitoon denial. End of story.

Taoiseach Hislop has spoken. Arkins?

Arkins *ponders.*

Taoiseach (*patronising*) Arkins will ingest. Arkins will digest. Arkins will relieve himself of his burden.

Arkins Taoiseach?

Taoiseach Arkins?

Arkins Elizabeth the First and Grace O'Malley at Taraford – I'd say it was waiting to happen.

Taoiseach Your point?

Arkins It's so *you*, Taoiseach. If it hadn't happened, we'd have had to make it up!

Taoiseach You're not slow! You describe to a T the weather they create!

Arkins Or, simply stated, they've arrived exactly on cue!

Taoiseach Are these women for real, Arkins?

Arkins Unquestionably.

Taoiseach So what are you saying? Ghosts? Revenants? Strays from the ether?

Arkins Strays, charged particles, succubi – call them anything you like. All they ask – and God knows it's little enough – is to be treated warmly.

Taoiseach In short?

Arkins I'm agog.

Taoiseach As am I. Truly. Spin-Doctor Hislop is not agog. That frisson awaits him.

Hislop (*snarl*) Does it now!

Taoiseach Hislop, I understand your hesitations – these women, yes, are volatile, but *not* in the way you think. They're volatile because – as Arkins has spotted – they're bona fide. That confirms my intuition, and, it follows, as night the day, the high necessity is to rejoice in them, and – *and* – get them comprehensively on-side. Widen your gaze, Hislop, can't you envisage them as windfall, shimmering flotsam, a luscious invitation to –

Hislop Lulu-land! Taoiseach, with respect, tie a knot in your Member of the Lower House, pillage your medicine-cabinet for a strong depressant, swallow it or eat it or insert it or kneel down before it, and leave me, like a dacent man, to deal with these wagons. That or I resign. I can take anything except another season of adolescent fantasizing.

Hislop *to the window. Uproar from the horses on the lawn.* **Hislop** *starts throwing apples to them (bin handy). Uproar increases.* **Hislop** *takes to* firing *apples at the innocent creatures, which retreat in noisy disarray.* **Hislop** *remains at the window, cooling his jets.* **Taoiseach** *has been parading downstage with* **Arkins**, *the two engaged in easy conversation – inaudible during* **Hislop**'s *window cameo but now happily available to us.*

Taoiseach It's the poet in you understands, that's why I've always said, 'Have a poet on the premises.'

Arkins A look sufficed, Taoiseach. They're a summons to …the Beyond!

Taoiseach *Beyond the Beyond!*

Arkins And that, surely, is the whole point!

Taoiseach Meaning?

Arkins The sensualist within – *must* be released – however we manage it!

The **Taoiseach** *embraces* **Arkins**, con moto. **Hislop**, *surly, joins them.*

Hislop   Forgive the tantrum, Taoiseach. But one poor enquiry, if I may. Why is everyone getting so excited over two floozies?

Arkins   (*quietly*) Floozies they are not!

Taoiseach   Hislop, have a care! How dare you impugn my motives in extending a provisional welcome to these visitors. They are – to my impartial eye – well-furbished women of the world, *some* world; their credentials merit the closest scrutiny. Optimum reading? The greatest English sovereign ever – and our pirate of legendary prowess – select Taraford for pleasure-ground and the Irish Head of State for confidante. I can go with that. These women have a contribution to make, and I intend to give them scope. I know the citizens of this island, Hislop. They *demand* the hubbub of event. Without it, they look starved, *are* starved. That, Sir, is the insidiously abiding germ of blight in the soul of the Gael, and I, for one, will not be party to its propagation!

Hislop   A fresh slant on the Famine. Great! Meanwhile, what's to be done with these leftovers from the last Paddy's Day Pageant?

Taoiseach   Hislop! I have – conferred – with my guests, singly and together, in the most civilised and leisurely fashion. The exchanges, I can tell you, were remarkably open. I found no reason to doubt the credentials of these rounded marvels. I am convinced, as Arkins there beside you is convinced, that their arrival here is purposeful *and* replete. I am now going to join them, leaving you, Sir, to the mercies of the flat-footed, constipated, and suety Constable who – it appears – has commandeered the zone which, in you, passes for understanding.

Taoiseach *exits, with purpose, through the door last used by* **Elizabeth**.

Hislop Now where are we?

Arkins Where men delight to play!

Hislop You're infected – aren't you?

Arkins Who wouldn't be? Don't you think it's amazing?

Hislop Have you taken leave of your –

Arkins I'm being invited to take leave of the mundane world – politics, appointments, disappointments, traffic-jams, breathalysers, income tax, the lot – and I accept! O, taste and see, man!

Pause.

Hislop What are *succubi*?

Enter **Sheridan**.

Arkins *Succubus*, singular, *succubi*, plural. They move, it seems, between the worlds. Voraciously! Upright, on all fours, missionary, sixty-nine, plain old welcome-home-sailor, marathon or quickie, infinite variety their signature and seal. Ever come across one, Sheridan?

Sheridan I was just going to say, I believe I saw them jig-antikin in the grounds, Mr A.

Hislop The women?

Sheridan The same pair, Mr H.

Hislop When did this circus erupt?

Sheridan First I knew of it was this mornin', Mr H.

Arkins How has he been?

Sheridan His normal self, Mr A.

Hislop His *normal* self?

Sheridan Approximatin' to normal, Mr H. Figayrey is, ye see, he's not normal, as ye know, unless he's a wee bit sod-off-the-load. At the same time, funny enough, he'll ate no clocks.

Hislop Sheridan?

Sheridan Mr H?

Hislop Find the Taoiseach, tell him we're waiting to see him. Mc Phrunty could be with us within hours, and, besides, there's a rake of enquiries and engagements to be dealt with.

Sheridan Done, Mr H.

Exit **Sheridan**.

Hislop Grandstanding apart, why are you encouraging him – this – these rips?

Arkins It's quite simple. I love him near the edge –
when he steps out of himself he's – I can't take my eyes
off him. And the women!

Hislop I thought you were gay.

Arkins Indeed. And that means I'm entirely open to
temptation.

Hislop What was it you said they were?

Arkins *Succubi*. Shoe-horn shoo-in succubi.

Hislop Why've I never heard of *succubi*?

Arkins They're one of the great unmentionables.

The two sit, **Arkins** *excited,* **Hislop** *sombre.*

Hislop They just *move in*?

Arkins That's it, by all accounts.

Hislop And the fun begins?

Arkins Exactly.

Hislop (*morose*) One of the great unmentionables …

Arkins I'd a granduncle lived with one twenty years.

Hislop Really? Where?

Arkins Donnycarney. Two up, two down. Tax
inspector.

Hislop Thrived?

Arkins Summer in Paradise, I'm told. Lived to ninety.
She left the week he died. *They* can't age. Seems.
Dorothy, the name was.

*Rattle of the crows out there, first we've heard of them.
Light quieting. The two sit,* **Arkins** *agog. From* **Hislop** *a
large sigh. He looks bleakly at the audience, changes vein,
rises, determined.*

Hislop Shite an' onions!

Arkins What is it now?

Hislop They're piss-flaps on the make.

Arkins Back to that?

Hislop Spaced-out snatches. A security lapse. Throw
them the few quid if we have to. I've no problem with
that.

Arkins 'Security lapse' is good. (*Smiling happily*) I like
that. 'Security lapse'…

*Melodious baying of a wolfhound from the lawn. The two
listen.*

Ribald whinnying of a horse. The two listen.

*Dangerously mundane clatter of the crows. The two sit
there, pensive.*

ACT ONE
SCENE FOUR

Lute notes – why not? – to let us know the delights in store. Enter **Elizabeth** *and* **Grace**, *the door, as always, humbly cooperative.*

Elizabeth *Bon matin, mes enfants, bon matin!*

Grace How's the men? What's the crack, tell us?

The males rise, unsure of what's next and with good reason. The women, altogether commanding, take over. Two areas of simultaneous action develop. One will feature **Elizabeth** *and* **Hislop**, *the other* **Grace** *and* **Arkins**.

Elizabeth/Hislop *She takes him by the hand, leads him downstage left. Next she positions him so that the two are standing together in conversational mode,* **Elizabeth** *brimming with seduction,* **Hislop** en garde *and then some. Locking eyes with her prey,* **Elizabeth** *lets her beautiful upstage hand drift to her cleavage, dally there, and, from that sweet nest, she fetches a lime-green apple. She admires the apple, kisses it, listens to it.*

Elizabeth (*to the apple*) *Vraiment?*

She glances at **Hislop**, *apple now resting on her palm, extends her palm with its precious cargo.*

Elizabeth Touch it.

29

Hislop *studies* **Elizabeth**, *studies the apple, makes no move.*

Elizabeth   Touch it.

Hislop *studies* **Elizabeth**, *studies the apple, makes no move.*

Elizabeth   No?

Hislop *studies the apple, glances over his shoulder to see what's happening elsewhere. He looks to the audience and back to the apple. He makes no move, stares at the apple.* **Elizabeth** *polishes the apple lazily against her belly. She makes a meal of that. He can't take his eyes off the action. She again extends the shining prize.*

Elizabeth   (*softly*) Touch it. (*He does.*)

Elizabeth, *at once, sets up a table and two chairs. The two settle.* **Elizabeth** *produces a gleaming knife. She peels and slices the apple, feeds* **Hislop** *as you'd feed the hungry (on whom you have designs).*

Meanwhile, **Grace** *has taken* **Arkins** *downstage right. She positions him (standing) at a table, stands facing him, takes out the pack of cards.*

Grace   (*aside to audience*) Deck stacked – but shure isn't that life?

She next drops on to the table a clinking purse – all her savings, clearly. **Arkins** *views the challenge, flings his wallet on to the table.*

Grace   Yer one brave lad!

They play Pontoon, at speed. **Grace** *wins, collects the loot on the table, deals again, wins again. She whips* **Arkins'** *shirt off his back, deals again, wins again, whips off his trousers. She deals again, wins again, whips off his underpants. She studies him.*

Grace   (*to audience*) Christ, but he sthrips horrid well! The poet Arkins (*this to him*). Yer not from Limerick, I hope?

That line is the cue for the **Taoiseach** *entering the auditorium. He's clearly troubled. His focus is on the audience, and he has a certain bother in choosing a place from which to address them. While that's being resolved, he allows himself occasional bemused glances towards the stage action. He sees it and doesn't see it, you'd say. Finally he finds a position that's to his satisfaction, addresses the audience. What we get from him is a series of interjections rather than sustained speech. It's a staccato confession, really.*

Taoiseach   *A chairde* – I believe I may have made a mistake … I may be wrong in this … but I believe … I'm sure you know the feeling … I believe – I may have made a possibly irretrievable mistake … It's just a hunch …

He leaves slowly, now and again glancing dazedly at the audience, the stage; the **Arkins/Grace** *and the* **Elizabeth/Hislop** *duets have been proceeding merrily.*

Arkins   Cork. Limerick a no-no?

Grace A posterior opening through which Ireland relieves herself. I met a couple of poets – London go-boys – in me travels. Fella called Ben Jonson – sez I, 'You couldn't be a poet, your mouth too closely resembles your anus.' True! Never forgave me. An' I met Will Shakespeare, young fella clearin' away horse-dung outside the Globe Theatre, I believe it was called. 'Not much of a job,' says I. 'Fella has to start somewhere,' says he, cool as ye like, an' him eyeing me up and down, mostly down. We had some good times. Did well at the writin', didn't he, after? Jesus, ye sthrip horrid well, Arkins!

Arkins *bows.* **Elizabeth** *joins them, inspects* **Arkins'** *enticements (***Hislop** *is hovering over the pile of* **Arkins'** *clothing).*

Elizabeth (**Grace** *alongside her, admiring* **Arkins**) Arkins, Arkins, where have you been all the days, where have you been the starved seasons long! Had I a sword handy, I'd knight you on the spot, by Our Lady I would!

Grace Horrid well, Arkins, doesn't he sthrip horrid well, Liz?

Elizabeth (*tantrum*) O'Malley!

Grace What?

Elizabeth Why, why, why under benign dispensation of the stars, *must* you, without let, abuse my native tongue so? *Horrid well* – what can that possibly mean? I heard you saying the other day, 'I'm not as green as I'm cabbage-looking, y'know' – what can that gibberish

mean? When I enquired, you yourself were quite
unable to satisfactorily explain, you –

Grace It *can't* be explained.

Arkins It's too eloquent, Majesty, to be explained.

Grace It means just what it says – 'I'm not as green' –

Elizabeth 'As you're *cabbage-looking*'?

*While that's going on, Hislop (low-key) has been
encouraging* **Arkins** *to resume his clothing, without success.*
Arkins *finds time to get some glasses of quality white wine
moving.* **Grace, Elizabeth,** *and* **Arkins** *clink glasses.*

Arkins To cabbages!

Grace And Queens!

Hislop *now seeking to make a getaway discreetly.*

Elizabeth Hislop, Hislop – nay, don't creep away,
tarry a while, Hislop!

Hislop *returns.* **Arkins** *serves him a glass of white. This is
the cue for the* **Taoiseach,** *unnoticed, to slip onstage
(French window) and settle unobtrusively in a marginal
chair. From there he studies the action with fevered
attention, not missing a syllable.*

Elizabeth We are enjoying, I should in honesty say it
out, our first visit to this strange island. My father
seldom spoke well of it, as you may be aware. There is
on record his famous description of it as 'the womb
with a view'.

Grace *has taken* **Hislop** *away for a chat. They promenade, apart.*

Arkins 'The womb with a view'!

Elizabeth A taking conceit?

Arkins I can – I believe – see what he was getting at, Majesty.

Elizabeth And on another celebrated occasion – Hoyden goes into a passion when I mention this – he described your compatriots, dear Arkins, as 'that nation of herdsmen, they know the rump-steak in the bullock as the Greeks the statue in the marble!'

Arkins And never, Majesty, said a truer word!

Elizabeth Arkins?

Arkins Majesty?

Elizabeth What, stir my memory, was that phrase Hoyden used of you a moment ago?

Arkins O – 'sthrips horrid well', Majesty.

Elizabeth And that's *Gaelic*, do I take it, for *très seduissant*?

Arkins *Precisement*, Majesty.

Elizabeth (*petting him*) You, Poet Arkins, shtrip horrid well!

Elizabeth extends her right hand for an adoring kiss.
Naked **Arkins** *genuflects, obliges, no better man. The two*
now sit, drink, talk sotto voce. *Meanwhile,* **Grace** *has*
been doing a number on Hislop. For starters, the
Elizabeth/Arkins *cameo in full flow, she feeds him the*
remaining slices of apple. Then she has him take her on a
tour of the pictures of the **Taoiseach**. *He will give her all*
the fascinating background. They admire, they converse
sotto voce, **Grace** *in great form,* **Hislop** *gradually losing*
it. As **Elizabeth** *and* **Arkins** *shift to quiet mode,* **Grace**
and **Hislop** *move to audibility.*

Grace Isn't Elizabeth extraordinary, Hislop?

Hislop *nods, wary.*

Grace Enjoy the apple?

Hislop *ditto.*

Grace But, sweet Jesus, she's Star of the Sea beautiful!

Hislop *ditto.*

Grace Know what it is, Hislop?

Hislop *shakes his head, wary.*

Grace She has *haunches*, Hislop, by the Lord Harry
she has *haunches!*

Hislop *nods, wary.*

Grace You've remarkable eyes, Hislop, anyone ever
tell you that?

Hislop *shakes his head, wary.*

Grace Restful eyes.

Hislop *nods, dubious.*

Grace 'Sleepsome', I calls them.

Hislop *looking about for help.*

Grace *Undertaker* eyes, I think I mean, honest, ready, cleansin' …

Hislop *watching it.*

Grace No side. Whatsomeever. 'Sorry for yer trouble, oak or deal?'

Grace *drifts a hand to her décolletage, searches, no, then remembers, switches hand to her profuse, dark, and healthily shining black hair, lets the hand wander there.* **Hislop** *watches, trapped. Quick move,* **Grace** *produces from her hair a small, brightly coloured, exuberantly writhing snake, which she displays, close-up, to* **Hislop**, *then tucks into her décolletage.* **Hislop** *staggers, sits, cue for the* **Taoiseach** *– enough's enough – to rise and intervene.*

Taoiseach (*advancing*) Why didn't someone tell me there was a party?

Grace Shure we forgot!

Taoiseach *tours, close inspection of* **Hislop**, *followed by scornful circling of* **Arkins** *(who remains cool).*

Arkins   Taste of the vino, Taoiseach?

This gallant offer is now acknowledged. **Taoiseach** *moves downstage, gazes, Arctic of visage, into the future.*

Taoiseach   May I be alone with my guests?

Exit **Arkins** *and* **Hislop**.

Musical whinnying of the horses, musical fade, and low-key piano 'I dreamt that I dwelt …'

ACT ONE
SCENE FIVE

The women sit, wonderfully relaxed. **Taoiseach** *paces, troubled, decidedly. Extend hiatus to the limit.*

Elizabeth Well, shouldn't the scene begin? Clearly, there's going to be a *scene*!

Taoiseach *not listening, continues fretful pacing.*

Grace I like Arkins. I swear to God his teeth are *bevelled*! And I thought I'd seen it all!

Elizabeth (*petting her beautiful right hand*) A peacock – that I sought to fondle – pecked my hand.

Grace The Royal Whinge. Next stop Wars of the Roses!

Elizabeth World will unerringly savage what one values most. (**Taoiseach** *halts, stares at* **Elizabeth**, *caught between fascination and seething suspicion*) In my case (*she displays her hands*) these – inherited from my mother – Boleyn hands. All my life they've been under attack – wasps, parrots, dogs, jennets. Bloody Mary threatened to chop them off. Maybe I should wear gauntlets – but that would be to hide my treasure, and God spare me from such surrender. I am not a Lion but I am a Lion's cub and I own a Lion's heart!

Taoiseach Who are you?

Elizabeth You have doubts?

Taoiseach I think it wonderful that you're here – both of you – but I must know who – and what – you are.

Elizabeth (*snap*) We are what we are. Reflect, Sir, on your good fortune. Do you think it accident that, being who I am, I'm here, Grace O'Malley by my side? Our appearance here has nothing to do with your place in history? Your sense of destiny? Do you conceive of me and your compatriot – that sweet salt-bleached hoyden – as minions of some rump keen to impair you? Or – *spit it out* – are we to you mere echoes, figments, cow-eyed syllabubs?

Taoiseach 'Syllabubs'?

Grace Frothy shamshite, Taoiseach.

Elizabeth Is that your airy reckoning?

Taoiseach Majesty – Elizabeth –

Elizabeth 'Bess'?

Taoiseach Thank you. 'Bess'. Are you an actor? Is this some inspired performance? Just let me know – give me an –

Grace 'Apersooh' – in the parleyvooh?

Elizabeth *Aperçu? Surement.* Am I an actor? Yes. Aren't you? You flex those inestimable legs, flaunt your profile, the dovecots flutter, ache, and sigh. Performance! Where, Rucksack, will it land us? Who cares? I deem adventure the very sap of life, what rouses us of a morning, steers the saucy day, candles the dusk, conducts us to the palpitating boudoir and the couch of pleasure in the urgent light and shade of damn'd be him – or her – who cries *Hold, enough!*

Grace   Now yer thrashin', Lizzie!

Pause. Cheerful prattle of the crows audible.

Taoiseach   I believe you. I believe I do believe you. And now, Bess, Grace, I need your help in resolving a small local contretemps.

Elizabeth   God's truth, he's not back to his bloody heave! Talk to him, Grace, I'll do my yoga.

Elizabeth *to the floor, commences her exercises. At intervals she'll give us,* sotto voce, *'Ommm, ommm, ommm, padmi humm'. There are regular complicated breathing sounds.* **Grace** *takes the* **Taoiseach** *for a companionable arm-in-arm stroll.*

Grace   Taoiseach, j'ever hear the story, I was fifteen, wandering Clare Island, an eagle pounced, took me, departed trumpeting, ever hear that story?

Taoiseach   The sanitised version, yes, Grace protecting a lamb of the flock.

Grace   Lamb me arse. He came at me like Storm Force Ten.

Taoiseach   *Golden* eagle?

Grace   To be sure.

Taoiseach How beautifully in character. What was it like – the actual entering?

Grace A swoop. A splash. Gone.

Taoiseach Did it alter your life?

Grace Did it alter the eagle's? Carry a scar from it yet. What is it about scars, Taoiseach?

Taoiseach They remain.

Grace Shure isn't that it? And they need mindin'. Nothin' more dangerous than a lonesome scar.

Taoiseach 'Nothing more dangerous than a lonesome scar' – sometimes, Grace, your wisdom terrifies me!

Grace Kiss me scar, *a stór*, would ye?

She sweeps him to a couch. Both sit, **Grace** *tears at her clothing, hungrily.*

Grace Curse o' God, I'm thatched like an onion. *There* she is – sou'-west of the navel!

Taoiseach Eagle signature! *Veni, vidi, vici!*

Grace Kiss it, nuzzle it, *lick it for me*, will ye?

Taoiseach *obliges, and, at speed, the two are into a clinch. Heavy breathing, smooching.*

Elizabeth (*rising from the yoga*) Toolsack?

Grace Thanks, Bess.

Elizabeth (*as* **Grace** *tidies her clothing*) That signed photograph of François in the Long Gallery – dear, departed François, he was a friend?

Peacocks audible, crows move in, banish them.

Taoiseach (*catching breath*) Yes, indeed. Stayed here frequently. A great European. Huge loss. Irreparable. Really.

Grace François, me ould compadre!

Taoiseach You were acquainted?

Elizabeth To say the least.

Grace Used to call my scar *'The only Playboy of the Western World'*!

Taoiseach You met François – where? At the Elyseé?

Grace The sack mostly. He had his direct side.

Elizabeth What would you say of him, Trillock? They're claiming now, forsooth, that he was of a religious bent!

Grace *into skids of laughter.*

Taoiseach (*po-faced*) Difficult to say, really. I asked him once – 'François, do you believe in God?' We were in the grounds of his chateau, standing beside an evergreen oak approximately five hundred years old.

Grace I had him under that tree!

Elizabeth (*one-uppy*) Did you know, dear, of the love-
nest *in* the tree?

Taoiseach (*solemn plus*) 'I'm tempted,' he said, 'to
believe in God, but I find the concept of the
immortality of the soul rather embarrassing.' So
French!

Elizabeth That's him, that's him!

Grace (*mournful*) Lord protect us, I've only to think
of him, and –

Elizabeth Stop it, Grace!

Taoiseach Is she in some –

Grace (*fury*) The way he *faded* – why is it that's
allowed to happen in the world? It's *obscene*! Don't
speak to me, don't touch me, anyone!

Grace *isolates herself. Moanings on the rise.*

Taoiseach Can I get some –

Elizabeth It's just a fit.

Taoiseach Call a doctor?

Elizabeth We are our own doctors, Tayshine. She'll
get over it, it's as if a parch –

Taoiseach '*Parch*'?

Elizabeth Quite. A *parch* seizes her, a thirsty devil.
Comes and goes as pleases. Then, as you yourself

might say, Threesuck, 'What's life without its little addictions?' All right now, Grace?

Grace (*coming back to herself*) Sorry for the wirrastrua. François, yes, a *banquet* that man, *Taster's ten-course menu*, but just as much Olaf. My first lover, if you leave out the eagle. Young Swede. Fished him from the tide. We had no more nor six months together. The Burkes killed him. I waited. We swooped at nightfall, butchered the lot. Small blame if – at intervals – I glimpse blood. I am, God help me, the priz'nor o' remembrance!

Chilly clatter-squawk from the crows. The sun has gone in.

Taoiseach Well, yes, indeed ... Quite ... The Unforeseen, the ...

Elizabeth No matter. We met him, bedded him, buried him. Rest easy, François!

Taoiseach Such a big heart!

Elizabeth That's it, Tillsack! So *yielding* –

Grace Give ye his last drop, the poor divil.

Elizabeth His final breath!

Grace Think nothin' of it.

Elizabeth One of those men, as they say, would warm a coffin!

Grace Are you all right, *a mhic?*

The **Taoiseach** *is in difficulties.*

Elizabeth Threesock? Something awry?

Taoiseach No – just a slight stomach thing – I'll be –

Elizabeth Air?

Grace Salts? Brandy? Take a dander?

Taoiseach Yes, a walk abroad, perhaps – it's so close – will you excuse me, Ladies?

Elizabeth No more than a stroll, Trussock. *Everything in moderation,* as, I'm told, the ancients insisted.

Grace Take it aisy, *a stór.* An' if ye can't take it aisy, take it aisy as ye can.

Taoiseach *exiting.* **Taoiseach** *gone.*

Grace What they call – where I come from, Lizzie – 'the stannin' wakeness'!

Elizabeth The Irish have a word for it!

Grace I don't think that poor man is in his health.

Elizabeth But we have the cure for what ails him, Hoyden, we have the cure!

Elizabeth *to the piano. She plays; the two sing. The flavour is madrigal. It's (you can tell on the spot) their party piece.*

Elizabeth   One, two, three –

Both   (*singing*) Pussy drives the train/ Pussy rules the main/ Fuels too that passing jet/ And the global internet/ Puss-puss-pussy drives the train ... (*whirl of notes; verse two coming up*) Rules Venus, Pluto, crimson Mars/ And all motions of the stars/Have you, Sir, met Pussy yet/ There's a meeting few forget/ There's a meeting few forget ... (*whirl of notes; verse three coming up*) Bow your head, go on your knees/ Pray, pray to any God you please/ All they'll give you for your pain/ Is 'Pussy drives the train/ Pussy, Pussy, Puss-puss-pussy/ Mistress Pussy drives the train ...

And that seems to be that. But suddenly (as they say) the stage is crowded. The entire ensemble appear (this will include the wife and Mc Phrunty) and we soar into a showpiece chorale – with dance element. This (a reprise with wild variations of 'Pussy Drives the Train') is the musical director's chance of immortality and should not be missed. Note: the animals and the birds should not be left out of the vocals. They should, even, be given a gallop entirely to themselves. In short, it's a blast. This set-piece concludes Act I. *Nota Bene: An essential ingredient in the above is* (vid. Infra) *a particular shift. As soon as the celebratory thrust has been established, the colour of the proceedings should take a turn towards the troubling, the menacing, the chasm, i.e. sure, pussy drives the train, but pussy, by the same token, is high octane, and the mere lighting of a match has blown many away.*

ACT TWO
SCENE ONE

Enter the **Wife,** *dressing-gown, night-cap, mittens, slippers, hot whiskey, hanky handy, snifthering, all the signs of the flu – and yet a theatrical lift to the ensemble, and to her back-up gestural score, suggest that she's 'playing at' invalid and, further, that it's a role to which she's accustomed and which she can assume or discard as pleases. She inspects the room, specifically the pictures. They are, despite the* **Taoiseach***'s adjustments in Act I, again hanging askew. She finds an ornate walking stick (which, one suspects, has a symbiotic relationship with the pictures) and tours the collection, whacking them into line – or seeking that propriety. The effect of her attentions is, you'd say, merely to shift the skew from left to right. Nevertheless, when she inspects the exhibition after her assault, she seems happy with the result. She discards the walking stick, sits, sips her hot whiskey, presses a buzzer, and enter* **Sheridan.**

Wife   Have a drink, Sheridan.

Sheridan *fixes himself a whiskey; they clink glasses.*

Wife   *Saol fada!*

Sheridan   *Bás in Éireann!*

Sheridan *proceeds to busy himself going from door to door and industriously polishing the doorknobs. The wife watches this routine with a mix of fascination and delight.*

47

Wife Why – I've never asked you before, Sheridan – why do you keep polishing doorknobs?

Sheridan (*finishing the chore*) Saw an old butler doing it once, ma'am, an' me an apprentice. 'Keeps a body supple,' he told me.

Wife And, praise be, it's you that has the supple in ye, Sherry!

Sheridan Thank you, ma'am.

Doorknob stint over, he rejoins the wife.

Wife Where is everybody? What's happening? The heave? Mc Phrunty shafted?

Sheridan Divil the shafted. Shaftin' a-plenty, ma'am, but not me man.

Wife Tell me more.

Sheridan We've traffic, ma'am.

Wife Traffic! Thought as much. I can always smell traffic. Who is she?

Sheridan Two o' them in it, ma'am.

Wife Why not? Have they names?

Sheridan Oh, they've names all right, ma'am.

Wife Well? Are the names classified? *Top Secret?*

Sheridan Divil the secret, ma'am. Queen Elizabeth the First and Ms Grace O'Malley.

Pause.

Wife Queen Elizabeth?

Sheridan The very woman.

Wife The First?

Sheridan No resemblance to the Second, ma'am, none in the wide world.

Wife And – did you say – Grace O'Malley?

Sheridan Eggsackly, ma'am.

Wife The Pirate O'Malley, *Granuaile*, is it?

Sheridan That's her, ma'am. Smell the brine offa her.

Pause.

Wife Staying long, are they?

Sheridan No tellin', ma'am.

Wife No, I suppose not …

Sheridan But personally speakin' –

Wife Yes, Sherry?

Sheridan I don't somehow think they're for long under this roof.

Wife Why not?

Sheridan I wouldn't put money on it now, ma'am.
What I'm tryin' to say is – that pair, at the rate they're
going, 'll be taking off for Vaynus in a fiery chariot
before night, that's only *my* opinion now, mind ye, but,
to my notional ear, we won't have them on these
premises for long, ma'am.

Pause.

Wife Cherie?

Sheridan Still in the huff, ma'am.

Wife A muff in a huff. Dear, dear. Life is so – what is
it, Sherry, so –

Sheridan Shlithery, ma'am.

Wife *Shlithery*, Sheridan, that's very good, very good!
Come here, Sheridan. Give me a shlithery kiss, would
you?

The two enjoy an ample kiss.

Wife (*glass aloft*) As long as I have my supple
Sheridan, I wouldn't call the queen me aunt!

*Merrily she tours the pictures, stick in hand, whacking
them back into the skewed positions she left them in a
while ago. And repeat of* **Sheridan**'s *doorknob routine –
it's becoming more sexualized by the second.*

Wife Hislop and Arkins around, Sherry, to help with
'The Dignitaries'?

Sheridan Here this while, ma'am. Havin' a great time.

Wife Group-grope? Orgy? Positions undreamt of?

Sheridan Early days, ma'am. Mr A is flyin', Mr H pale 'round the gob, last time I saw him.

Wife Mc Phrunty – 'The Inflated-in-Waiting'?

Sheridan Talk of him comin', ma'am. The women'll ate him alive, ma'am, if they're still here – and they will – when he gets here – if he gets here –

The **Wife** *goes to the piano, gives us the opening bars of 'I Dreamt that I Dwelt in Marble Halls'.* **Sheridan** *strikes a* **Taoiseach** *strut and begins to sing, voice a mix of mock-Irish tenor and the* **Taoiseach**'s *familiar voice.*

Sheridan I dreamt that I dwelt in marble halls, with vassals and serfs by my side/ And of all who assembled within those halls, that I was the hope and pride ... (*The music continues low-key;* **Sheridan** *shifts to* **Taoiseach**'s *speaking voice*) ... I dreamt that I dwelt – heard it first at the grandmother's knee – she had it from Balfe himself, he worshipped her young beauty! Used to speak, she told me, of the composer Field, *our* Chopin. Field, who, as many of you will know, died in exile, wrote to him once – 'I arrived in Moscow with only two friends, the cold, and the unknown.' We are doomed, I've said it before, to destroy our bravest and best. Exile them to some freezing desert or, as suits, crucify them on home turf, under, need I say, the guise of Due Process!

The **Wife** *applauds;* **Sheridan** *bows.*

Wife You're a star, Sherry. You should be declared a National Treasure. Encore!

The **Wife** *resumes at the piano and, together, the two resume,* con moto, *the mock-***Taoiseach** *rendering of the Balfe song, only to be interrupted. Door opens. It's* **Hislop.**

Hislop Apologies, ma'am.

Wife Come in, come in.

Hislop (*advancing*) Any sign of our guests, Sheridan?

Sheridan Didn't see hide nor hair o' them this while, Mr H.

Hislop In the grounds, do you fancy?

Sheridan More nor likely, Mr H.

Hislop Thanks.

Exit **Hislop,** *preoccupied. But he has an aside for the audience as he leaves (by a door opposite his point of entry).*

Hislop I don't know who they are – what they are. All I know is they must be captured alive. And then? No idea.

Exit **Hislop.**

Wife Sherry?

Sheridan Ma'am?

Wife If you'd be so kind, 'The Dew on the Rose'.

Sheridan Certainly, ma'am.

She waves him into action. **Sheridan** *parades, moves into* **Taoiseach** *strut, demeanour.*

Wife 'They used to say of François' –

Sheridan (*bow, collusive*) They used to say of my dear friend François, well, they said many things of him, great European that he was, connoisseur of *la vie sensuelle* in all its faucets …

Wife 'Facets' –

Sheridan 'Facets'?

Wife You're right! 'Faucets.'

Sheridan Connoisseur of *la vie sensuelle* in all its faucets …

Enter **Taoiseach.**

Taoiseach (*to* **Sheridan**) Have you seen my guests?

Sheridan In the grounds, more nor likely, Taoiseach. Mr H came through here a minute ago lookin' for them.

Taoiseach Did he now? Have we a convert on our hands!

Wife Manicurist? Gone shopping? Gym? Anyone for tennis?

Taoiseach *disregards that, heads for the door used by* **Hislop***, pauses, goes to his wife, perfunctory kiss, exits per chosen door.* **Sheridan** *and the* **Wife***, in sync, wave silent goodbyes to departing* **Taoiseach***.* **Sheridan** *steadies, resumes his recitation.*

Sheridan   They used to say of François, that he had the quality of 'the dew on the rose'. I first heard that standing in the grounds of his chateau under an evergreen oak at least five hundred years old. What is that exquisite phrase intended to convey? I will tell you. By 'the dew on the rose' is meant that you could wonder over him, ceaselessly admire, ceaselessly study, but you could never *seize* him, never, ever, could you *seize* the man. (*Pause*) The *dew on the rose cannot be seized!* (*Pause*) I would, some day, please God, like to have that said of me – 'He resembled *the dew on the rose*'.

The **Wife** *applauds.* **Sheridan** *bows.*

Wife   (*impish*) So true, isn't it?

Sheridan   Ma'am?

Wife   (*with active gestural score*) That dew – on the rose – can't get hold of it, can you?

She finds a rose. Going to the window, scissors in hand, snip-snip from a convenient rose-bush, returns with this trophy, examines it closely, gives **Sheridan** *the chance to assist in this seizing of the 'dew on the rose'. It can't be done, turns out or, at best, it's hellishly difficult. Make their endeavours into a choreographic cameo of lovers play-acting before going to bed. When it seems right, they exit. They're going, going, gone to bed.*

ACT TWO
SCENE TWO

Taoiseach *on. Decidedly on edge. Snaps out of that, tours the room, sniffing, sniffing …*

Taoiseach My wife and my ever-obliging butler are now in bed together – the ravenous two-backed beast! Well, I suppose they could be at worse. What she sees in him – perhaps he has a big cock? Does size matter? If they tell you it doesn't, they're lying. *Where, in Christ's name, are my guests?* Sheridan is given to garlic – but he has great stories. The one about the day he was thumbing – Navan area, and, foggy day, doesn't he thumb a *hearse*, super-model. 'What'd you do, Sheridan?' 'Skipped over a ditch, Taoiseach.' Or the one about his father – who, seems, had what they call in the hills 'a grand lovely voice'. People always asking – 'Where'd you get a voice like that, Packy?' 'I don't know – but I'll tell ye one thing, it was *dear bought*.' I'll remember that story if I live to be a hundred. Which I won't. *Where are my guests?* I could *eat* them, I admit it. Breakfast, dinner, tea, midnight supper, three a.m. supplement, extensive dawn *petit repas* … But also, I know, as previously acknowledged, I am making – I may be wrong, it's possible I have it wrong – but I believe I'm making a mistake. An irretrievable mistake. (*Exiting now, but he pauses to give us another blast*) And here's the question that knifes me – doesn't it ever spear you? – why is there such pleasure, limitless pleasure, in the full knowledge of, full consent to, disaster?

Exits.

ACT TWO
SCENE THREE

We hear the lazy fingering of a lute, 'Greensleeves'.
Hislop, Arkins *and* **Sheridan** *wander on. It should be as though they were here all the time, only invisible – that flavour.* **Hislop** *at a bookshelf,* Encyclopaedia Britannica, *volume after volume gleaming there. His searching fingertips find a particular volume (S for* succubi*?). He takes it down, riffles pages, finds an entry and, sitting on a chair-arm, begins anxiously to read.* **Arkins** *is seated, studying his left palm. Pen in hand, he's marking (with loving care) the various lines that come to his attention.* **Sheridan** *is quietly going about his butler chores, checking stocks of drink, polishing glasses, so on. The atmosphere is brittle. A glass may well explode at any moment.*

Arkins A famous palmist read Oscar Wilde's palm, Paris period, late on. The palmist had no idea – curtain, hand through an aperture – who his client was. Right palm studied, left palm. The palmist spoke. 'These are the palms of a king. A king who has been sent into exile.'

Hislop It says here there's no proof that *succubi* exist. It's 'widely held' that they exist. Doesn't go beyond that.

Arkins 'A king who has been sent into exile' – what's the Irish for masturbate, Hislop?

Hislop *shrugs, absorbed above the* Encyclopædia Britannica, *Volume S.*

Only an Apple

Arkins *Sinn Féin!* And for *cunnilingus?*

Hislop *still removed,* **Sheridan** *tuned in.*

Hislop They exist, and they don't. That's my life!

Arkins Sheridan? (**Sheridan** *puzzles*) *Deoch a' dorais!*

Sheridan *got that, likes it. Back to the brittle silence.*
Arkins *above his palm,* **Hislop** *pursuing his studies,*
Sheridan *is tempted by doorknobs and yields to*
temptation. Extend this hiatus to maximum. Now a
sound, a medley of sounds, intrudes from the lawn. At
first it scarcely impinges, but taking its own time, it
gathers force and cohesion. The animals – all the animals
– and the fowl – all the fowl – peacocks and crows in the
van, are giving voice. There's a concert en train. *The*
mélange is not discordant. On the contrary, it has a
haunting valedictory note at its heart. Gradually, all three
become aware of the 'concert', the strangeness of it. They
listen, in evident awe. They look at each other; they look
at the audience. The magical chorale – it has a magic –
lifts to another level of the elegiac valedictory. **Arkins**
(hesitating at first, as if not sure he has permission) begins
to tiptoe towards the open window. The others, consulting
(nods) needlessly with each other, follow him. All three are
now at the open window, but as they arrive the music
fades. The three look at each other, look back at the
audience, stand there in confusion.

Hislop (*to audience*) Lawn empty. Graveyard.

Arkins What an extraordinary concert!

Hislop We imagined it?

Sheridan No, Mr H, I heard it with me own two ears.

Arkins *motions them to silence. He's still listening, rapt.*

Hislop Our alleged *succubi* – extending their –

Arkins I'm afraid he's fucked.

Hislop (*thinking aloud*) Why is a woman – offering a tasty apple – a mortal threat?

Sheridan Th'animals – the birds – knows the know, I always heard.

Hislop Not to speak of a snake in her ring-a-lets.

The three coming downstage from the window.

Arkins They were saying good-bye, horses, hounds, birds, an uncomplicated, beautifully honest *slán abhaile*.

Sheridan Animals know – because they've no botherations, the mother always told me.

Hislop Maybe he *is* fucked – he'll go down fucking! That's him.

Arkins He told me last week, some gathering he attended, he walks into a room. A dog rose, basset-hound, quite deliberately rose, and walked out.

Hislop *Coitus interruptus* – there's an epitaph!

Arkins He was quite upset about it.

Sheridan Don't like them animals leavin', nor the
paycocks. Them too …

Sheridan *fixes recuperative drinks, things settle again,
kind of. But* **Hislop,** *fevered, drifts to the window, stands
there, looking out.* **Sheridan** *finds occupation polishing
vases. Their sumptuous curves deserve attention (to say the
least).* **Arkins** *is downstage, reflective/sombre.*

Arkins (*to audience*) Maybe – auditory hallucination
– it happens, maybe we – communally – imagined the
whole thing? (*He stands there, distracted*) I love
Elizabeth's story about her dad and Ireland – 'the
womb with a view'. Was that a novel by –

Brash knock on the door, door opening. Enter Mc Phrunty.

Hislop Mr Mc Phrunty –

Mc Phrunty I hope we don't intrude, Gintlemen?

All four go into wild laughter.

Hislop Sean, you're welcome. You know Arkins?

Arkins Morning, Sean.

Mc Phrunty You're the poet – ye *look* the poet.

Arkins What look is that, Sean?

Mc Phrunty And that's Sheridan – we met before.
What's a poet look like, Sheridan?

Sheridan You tell us, Mr A.

Arkins *'Death to love one, death to marry one, death to be one!'*

Jittery acclamation.

Sheridan Drink, Mr Mc P?

Mc Phrunty Mineral water, thanks.

Hislop Taoiseach here any second, Sean. Looking forward, hugely, to consultations.

Mc Phrunty I know. Met him down the corridor.

Sheridan Still or sparkling, Mr Mc P?

Arkins Alone?

Mc Phrunty In a hurry.

Hislop Give the man a *drink*, Sheridan, will you?

Arkins Anyone with him?

Mc Phrunty Excited. But sure we all get excited. Good for the gizzard.

Sheridan (*supplying*) JJ&S, Mr Mc P.

Mc Phrunty Thanks, Sheridan. Happy Days in Killaloe!

Chorus Happy Days ... *Sláinte* ... *Saol fada* ...

Mc Phrunty He looked – he looked hard at it – goin' for it – foot on the –

Sheridan Martyr for the jiminasticks, Mr Mc P.

Hislop Morning racket-ball, likely.

Arkins Play yourself, Sean?

Mc Phrunty Play? What?

Arkins (*jokey*) Games?

Mc Phrunty Whist only.

Sheridan *Whisht, whisht –*

Hislop Whisht what?

Sheridan They're comin'. I've ears like a fox.

Door opens (of its own accord, opens 'dramatically') and enter **Taoiseach, Elizabeth,** *and* **Grace.** *Change for the* **Taoiseach** *shirt, shorts, sandals. This man exudes, as they say, well-being, beckoning horizons. He could be a Medici on speed.*

Taoiseach Sean – there you are – watered and foddered? Meet my guests, Her Majesty, Queen Elizabeth the First – my friend and colleague, Sean Mc Phrunty –

Elizabeth We are pleased, good Mc Phrunty, pleased indeed –

Mc Phrunty Your Majesty –

Taoiseach And Grace O'Malley –

Grace Sean, *Dia dhuit, a mhic* –

Mc Phrunty Pleasure, Ms O'Malley, great pleasure …

Taoiseach Party time! Champers, wine, the hard stuff. To it, Sheridan! Hang sangers comin' up!

Immediate buzz, clink of bottles and glasses, and we have **Taoiseach** *and Mc Phrunty downstage in excited conversation.*

Taoiseach Sean, Ould Stock, delighted you could make it. Time – surely – for a gosther?

Mc Phrunty Why I'm here, Taoiseach. Who're the women?

Taoiseach (*turning to admire his prizes*) The women? The women are – magnificent! Buttocks like the Greeks! And now *you* are here. Which completes my happiness. So long as conversations are taking place, there's no vacuum. Vacuum invites mayhem. Mayhem invited hokum. And therefore God made ganders and the grease-gun got lost of a Tuesday! What do you think, Sean?

Mc Phrunty *glances upstage, measuringly.*

Mc Phrunty *Thearaticals*, are they?

Taoiseach Sean, Sean, *Sean* – make the jump, man! Know what they say about you in The House? 'Mc Phrunty can't think on his feet. And when he sits down, it's worse.' I disagree. I think it's better when you sit down. Much better. And why is that?

62

Mc Phrunty Lets you have the floor, Taoiseach!

Taoiseach Precisely. Listen, Sean – our two paragons – when they're around, I'm captive. When they're not, I'm *possessed*. Where, where have they gone? Riding? Swimming? Chess? Meditation? Does she walk or does she sit or does she – know the feeling, Sean?

Mc Phrunty I have the numbers, Taoiseach.

Taoiseach But will they add up? Nub of the hub, Sean, is my guests asked hungrily to meet you – Grace close to fever – what marvels is she sitting on over there? Can I be frank, Sean? She wants quality time with you.

Mc Phrunty Who? What?

Taoiseach Grace. With you. Now.

Mc Phrunty Shure I don't know the lassie from the pope's tooth.

Taoiseach Read about you. Collected pictures. Saw fit, even, to stalk. Truly.

Mc Phrunty How'd they land here?

Taoiseach Twenty-first century, Sean, Anything goes. Or hadn't you noticed?

Mc Phrunty What do they *want*, Taoiseach?

Taoiseach Here to help. Said so. Explicitly.

Mc Phrunty Debriefed?

Taoiseach *Debriefed?* Back, belly, and currabingoes. Squeaky clean.

Mc Phrunty I have the numbers, Taoiseach.

Taoiseach No, Sean. *They* have the numbers – in spades! Ladies, Majesty – Grace – come here, please, come here, *come*!

Elizabeth *and* **Grace** *join the two, and the* **Taoiseach** *obligingly wanders off.*

Grace Sean –

Mc Phrunty Yes?

Grace Don't expect too much of me now!

Elizabeth Next thing she'll be telling you she's shy, Shane.

Grace You look under strain, *a stór*. Your teeth, may I –

Mc Phrunty Me teeth?

Grace Just a look. (*He obliges*) Hmmm ... Grind your teeth, Sean?

Mc Phrunty Grind me – ?

Elizabeth *Not* an accusation, Shoon, she approves!

Grace I think it honest, why not grind if that's your itch?

Elizabeth Fellini did, Kipling, Victor Hugo –

Mc Phrunty   Mickey Mouse, Bo-Peep, the seventh
Dwarf –

Acclamation, laughter, ice broken.

Elizabeth   For that, Sir Mc Phrunty, you are awarded
a top-up. Goblet, please!

Elizabeth, *to the lilt of 'Greensleeves', vanishing with **Mc
Phrunty**'s glass.*

Mc Phrunty   Enjoyin' yer stay here, Ms O'Malley?

Grace   Grace, Sean, *please* …

Mc Phrunty   Grace – the mother was a Grace.
Enjoyin', Grace, the holiday?

The space has 'mysteriously' emptied of traffic. **Grace** *and*
Mc Phrunty *are alone. The lighting has gone wooingly
boudoir.*

Mc Phrunty   Where's everybody?

Grace   Who cares? Bowls. Snooker. Cares of office.
Hard to beat the bit of peace and quiet. *I love quiet.*
Take the weight off your croobs, Sean?

She leads him to an inviting couch. They sit.

Grace   You were askin'?

Mc Phrunty   Oh – yes – what was –

Grace   Was I enjoyin' the holiday? Answer: better,
much better, since *you* surfaced.

Mc Phrunty Why so?

Grace I love large men.

She casually fixes him a drink, replenishes her own, rejoins him on the couch.

Mc Phrunty Why so, Grace?

Grace Love large men?

Mc Phrunty Aye.

Grace Easier to keep track of! Been keepin' an eye on you, Sean. Stalked you, even.

Mc Phrunty So I'm told. Where?

Grace Golf-course. Bank. Religious services.

Mc Phrunty 'Religious services'?

Grace Why not? Forgotten you go to Mass on Sundays?

Mc Phrunty No, no –

Grace And I have a confession to make –

Mc Phrunty On with ye, on with ye – spill it –

Grace Sean – you – *kneeling to pray* –

Mc Phrunty What about it?

Grace *What about it?* You see! That's what makes it so – you don't know the *effect* – I've never seen anything

more sexy in my life! I take one look, *one*, and fuck-me
I'm a-brimmin'!

Mc Phrunty Why, Grace?

Grace The *erotic* – explain me the *erotic*, Sean! Hear
you're to be the next taoiseach?

Mc Phrunty (*modest*) I'll give it a shot, Grace.

Grace (*clink of glasses*) Road rise with you, Sean.
You've *leader* quality. In your shoulders, hams.

Mc Phrunty Time for a change – I think. Country
needs it. Fresh leadership – difficult times ahead –
GNP – a recession could hit like –

Grace *is weeping silently, happy tears, you'd hazard, but
tears nevertheless.* **Mc Phrunty** *is at a loss.*

Grace (*laughing through tears*) Don't mind me, Sean –
bear with me – I'll be all right in a –

Mc Phrunty *supplies hankies. They're used, tossed aside,
the tears continue. Sean to phone, retreats from phone.
The tears continue, copious, happy, but copious tears
nonetheless.* **Mc Phrunty** *to a door. Door stuck. He comes
back to* **Grace**. **Grace**, *recovering, has never looked more
beautiful.*

Mc Phrunty All right now, Grace? Jesus, I'm sorry –
did I say something outa turn – I'm sorry, Grace –

Grace Not at all, not at all, tear an' the smile, never
mind me, *a stór* –

Mc Phrunty   Yer grand now, are ye?

Grace   (*back to her commanding self*) I'm grand now, Sean, bar one thing.

Mc Phrunty   Can I help, Grace?

Grace   Yes, *a leanbh* – I believe you can. Just a little thing.

Mc Phrunty   Tell me. What is it? I'll be glad to –

Grace   Remember what I said about you kneeling – how mainsail, topsail, spinnaker *come-on* that was, *is*, sailin'-before-the-gale-abrimmin' – remember I told you about that –

Mc Phrunty   Aye –

Grace   Sean –

Mc Phrunty   Yes, Grace?

Grace   Sean, would you – if you don't want to it's fine – I understand, but – would you mind doin' it for me now – if it's not a bother –

Mc Phrunty   Doin' what, Grace?

Grace   That kneelin' – I can't explain it – it's *so* – could you do it for me again, Sean, now – please – I hope I'm not presumin' –

Mc Phrunty *looks about him, gathers his resources, goes on his knees, devout prayerful position.*

Grace *laps that up.*

Grace Sean, thank you – no – (*he's about to rise*) hould yer hoult a minute –

She goes to him, clawing at her clothing.

Grace Kiss me scar, Sean, will ye?

Mc Phrunty Grace –

Grace What?

Mc Phrunty I have the numbers, Grace.

Grace That's two of us, *a chroí*. Kiss me scar, will ye, it do get lonesome.

Mc Phrunty Where is it – the scar?

Grace There lookin' at yet, contaygious to the navel, kiss it, will ye, kiss it.

Mc Phrunty What gave ye that, Grace?

Grace Life, *a stór*. Kiss it, will ye, *kiss it*.

Mc Phrunty *kisses the scar, moans, groans, and rapid move to heavy-duty smooching, which* **Grace** *halts.*

Grace Sean, love –

Mc Phrunty Grace?

Grace Elizabeth –

Mc Phrunty   What about her?

Grace   She'll be waitin' for us. You. Me. The Mauve Room. Gave me strict orders. Take a dander, will we? Goin' on about ye for days … (*she's now escorting him towards a door*) … Beautiful, isn't she, those lion's cub eyelashes, were *you* smitten, *a mhic*? … I thought you were … We're terrible close, the pair of us …

Exit **Grace** *and* **Mc Phrunty**.

ACT TWO
SCENE FOUR

Consider lute chords, lascivious, as ushers to **Grace**
departing with her captive. Those chords are still playfully
present to welcome the **Taoiseach** *as he enters, inspects the*
room. He's fretful, uneasy, he's sniffing around. Quickly,
he's focused on the couch where **Mc Phrunty** *and* **Grace**
spent time. He sniffs his way unerringly from there to the
position where **Mc Phrunty** *knelt to kiss the pirate's*
delectable scar. Quizzical/fretful, he looks at the audience.
Goes to the piano, one finger japing, gives us a few notes
of 'I Dreamt that I Dwelt'. Drops that, goes again to the
couch, finds unerringly the exact spot honoured by **Grace's**
phidian buttocks, settles there, finds a rug handy, wraps
himself in the rug, and goes off to sleep, finger in mouth,
an anxious child.

Use the movement, and mitigation, of sunlight in the
space (and some more low-key lute sounds?) to convey the
passage of time and gathering tension. Enter the **Wife**,
with glass containing whatever, but steam rising busily
from it. She takes in the scene, goes straight to the couch,
positions herself beside it as for a photo-op. There's a
spectral (and altogether winning) bulb-flash from some
unknown imp.

Wife (*to audience*) The Picture of the Year!

She bows, exits, smiling.

The **Taoiseach** *comes to, removes his finger from his mouth, looks at it as if uncertain of ownership. He looks about, goes straight to one of the pictures, stares at it vehemently. The picture falls from the wall.*

Taoiseach (*to audience*) I just had a dream telling me that would happen.

He presses a buzzer. Enter **Sheridan**.

Sheridan Taoiseach?

Taoiseach Sheridan, Ould Sod – I think I may be losing the marbles.

Sheridan Don't be talkin' the like o' that now, Taoiseach. Shure ye're leppin' outa yer skin.

Sheridan *is efficiently setting the 'moving' picture against a wall.*

Taoiseach In a fatuous blaze of the sanguine, I offer two salivating vampires the run of my house. Not content with that, nothing will do me but throw Mc Phrunty into their laps. *The fire you light has to be controllable!* I keep seeing Kelly-green fire-buckets! What the hell is that about?

Sheridan *ponders a reply. We can hear him thinking.*

Taoiseach Say something, will you? Isn't that what you're paid for?

Sheridan (*to action*) About them ladies, Taoiseach –

Taoiseach *What?*

Sheridan Them – and Mr Mc P – shure they'll creel him while you'd slice a spud. It's *you* is the sun, the moon, an' the –

Taoiseach You cretin! Do you imagine I'm *jealous*?

Sheridan Never crossed me mind, Taoiseach.

Taoiseach I've never *had* to be jealous – because I always got what I wanted. *I know what I want*, say that for me. And *what I don't want*. These perambulating vulvas must be shown the door, then I can get back to work. Priorities? EU Presidency, National Pay Deal, my trip to Japan. (*taking off now*) I aim to climb Mount Fuji, take in some of the great temples, improve my knowledge of Japan's magnificent engravers, Hokusai, Utamaro, Enguchi … Sheridan?

Sheridan Taoiseach?

Taoiseach Why do they keep going on about death?

Sheridan Them engravers, is it?

Taoiseach My *guests*, man, this pair of black-widow spiders I'm landed with. My perfumed banshees! Everyone they've bedded is a corpse! All right, sex and death are the only topics – *are they?* – but this is necro – necro – what is it? – necro*SARCOPHAGI*!

Enter **Hislop**.

Taoiseach The women ministering to the Inflated-in-Waiting?

Hislop He is in their capable hands, Taoiseach.

Taoiseach Arkins?

Hislop General area of the *Mauve Room*, Taoiseach.

Taoiseach Clothed?

Hislop Clothed, Taoiseach, when last seen by me.

Taoiseach Hislop, I owe you an apology. (*Florid handshake, followed by florid embrace, which* **Hislop** *suffers awkwardly*) I am deeply sorry for any distress my obstinacy may have caused you. These creatures have to go. You will handle their departure.

Pause.

Taoiseach Have I said something wrong?

Hislop No, Taoiseach, no. But –

Taoiseach They've suborned stainless steel Hislop! I knew it!

Hislop Not at all, Taoiseach. But –

Taoiseach *BUT?*

Hislop *Will* they go, Taoiseach?

Taoiseach *Will they go?* You'd prefer me to deal with them? (*Nod from* **Hislop**. *The* **Taoiseach** *subjects him to a wicked glance*) Look at him! Fascination/repulsion written all over him! Well, at least, it shows you're human. Fine, leave them to me. A dangerous pair, I grant you, but I've opened – and closed – some tight boxes in my time. They'll play ball. Greased palm is the great mollifier. Their visit has had its moments. The massive plus is Mc Phrunty's sauce all over their bibs. We'll shunt him outa here with a warning. Poor ould sod, if he hasn't a future, at least he has the makings of a past.

Hislop's *nod indicates fragile assent.* **Sheridan** *serves drinks.*

Taoiseach   (*to audience*) An unfortunate aspect of our temperament is that the imagination easily takes fire. At times that works to the benefit of all. Other times it creates confusion. (*Beat*) Then, as has been noted, 'confusion is not necessarily an ignoble condition'!

A door opens of its own accord. Enter **Grace** *en deshabillé.*

Grace   How's the men, tell us? And the sultry live-long day a-hummin'?

The men stare.

Grace   Don't mind me, I know I'm only half-dressed. Lizbeth'll be here in a minute.

Taoiseach   ('*severe*') Will *she* be dressed?

Grace   ('*shocked*') Go back for me duds, is it?

Taoiseach   Hislop – Sheridan – Ms O'Malley and I will share a moment alone. And would you, Hislop, see that this young woman's companion is brought here at once.

Hislop   Certainly, Taoiseach.

Hislop *and* **Sheridan** *exit, the former treating the dishevelled* **Grace** *to a look which confirms the* **Taoiseach***'s reading that* **Hislop** *is on the hook.*

Grace (*pointing*) What happened the pore-trate?

Taoiseach *refuses to hear that. He's on his way to a convenience cupboard.*

Grace Took off, did it? Lookin' for to be *assumpted*, was it, or what?

Taoiseach *returning with a dressing-gown which he throws to* **Grace**.

Taoiseach Put that on – if you don't mind –

Grace Couldn't wait to strip me, now can't wait to wrap me up! O, the men's the bhoys! Shudda stayed with me eagle!

Taoiseach Put it on, please.

Grace (*sniffing the garment happily*) Yours begod! Can I keep it?

Wearing the garment, she frolics towards him to bestow a thank-you kiss and is sternly rebuffed.

Taoiseach Time, I'm afraid, for some tough talk.

Grace (*tickled*) 'Well now, the position is this'!

Taoiseach Listen to *me*, Grace – or Emir – or Molly – or whoever you are –

Grace Whisht!

Taoiseach Whisht *what*?

Grace Liz –

Taoiseach What about her?

Grace She's coming. I (**Grace** *looking fixedly at an already resonating door*) can see the hussy.

Taoiseach (*snarl*) Have you second sight?

Grace Aye, and twenty-second. Twenty-twenty twenty-second, *a leanbh*.

A door opens of its own accord. Enter **Elizabeth**, *triumphant*.

Elizabeth Teeside, he's now 'Sir Sean' – did Grace tell you? After the foreplay folderols I bestowed a knighthood. It seemed to us he was deserving of the honour – if only for his innocence!

Grace Gave *me* his Organ Donation Card, he did.

Taoiseach Gave you his *what*?

Elizabeth Last thing he said to me was – '*numbers*'. Just that one word, quite on its own.

Grace I was touched. Whole shebang donated – heart, liver, kidneys, eyes …

Elizabeth The sing-song word – '*numbers*' – it floated there like a lost –

Grace Chord?

Taoiseach Will the two of you – for one moment –
SHUT UP! I must point out –

Elizabeth 'Must!' *Must!* Little Man, the word *must* is
not used to princes!

Elizabeth *sweeps out, a door opening before her, closing
behind her.*

Grace Ye upset her now – an' everything goin' so well.

Taoiseach She's off the leash! See that flitther of her
fangs – and you're worse!

Grace Should I bate me breast?

Taoiseach I prefer *her*, she's honest about her venom
– but *you*, you're one of *us*, you'll soother and wheedle
and jook, then you'll sink the teeth!

Grace And, if I do, it's for mutual pleasure, as you
should be the first to know. Suffrin' Christ, I had such
faith in you. Now a hasky welt in the voice, and a
strainc on the puss, but at least I know the *why* of it.
Had his jollies, and my hayro is showin' streaks o' the
shakes. Met it so often it's not funny any more.
Mc Phrunty, God bless him, had a bit o' style! Did I
not tell you, he had a *céad míle fáilte* loss o'
consciousness?

Taoiseach Is he still in it?

Grace Just about – but not for long, I'd wager, gev
everythin', God bless him. *Everythin'*.

Taoiseach Should he be looked after?

Grace Isn't he after b'in' looked after, *a chro*? Wasn't I meself the one – as the three of us entered harbour – that gev him *The Mortal Kiss*?

Taoiseach *Mortal Kiss*?

Grace Aye, it's one of the sweetest explorations – for the likes of us, y'know – a stillness to it – and a softness – it's a sortov a lishpeen of a pógeen – God in Heaven, I wish I could *express* meself – ever feel, Taoiseach, that your willowy tongue – that lovely green offal – is just an upstart insubordinate, an upsthart unshubordinate dissolvin' solvint!

Elizabeth *arrives back.*

Elizabeth May I have a drink?

Taoiseach No.

Elizabeth How the mighty are fallen! A Tudor deemed a groundling!

Taoiseach I'm afraid I have to ask you both to leave. Sean was – is – you may not be aware – *Party Whip*. There could be a large demand on my time the next few days. Worst-case scenario, autopsy, lying-in-state, panegyrics –

Grace '*Pan-joy-ricks*' we used say around Westport!

Taoiseach Panegyrics and pathologists – you two don't really want any of that. So I'm afraid you'll have to leave. Quietly. Perhaps at some future date, God willing —

Elizabeth You mountebank!

Grace Cool it, Bess.

Elizabeth You mortified basket-case!

Grace Stuff a pratie in it, Boleyn, will ye?

Elizabeth Sir Swaddled Turd!

Elizabeth *sweeps out.*

Grace Good bloody riddance. Now, *a mhuirnín* –

Taoiseach Don't *a mhuirnín* me, Bitch-Box!

Grace All right. Start over. We're here be your invitation.

Taoiseach That is untrue.

Grace You've been howlin' for us for at least a decade. Besides, we never go nowhere unless we're invited.

Taoiseach How kind of you!

Grace And – it follies – we only *leave* as pleases, which seems fair. Ye see, Bess and I takes our responsibilities woeful serious.

Taoiseach And what responsibilities might *they* be, tell us?

Grace 'What in man doth woman most desire? The linyaments o' satisfied desire! What in woman doth man most desire? The linyaments – '

Taoiseach The pair of you *must* leave.

Grace Shure that's mighty. See ye on the lee-side when the wind modherates. All the sweeter for the delay, *a chuisle.*

Exit **Grace,** *walking slowly towards a door which, as we have learned to expect, opens to her advance. A metre or two from the door, she finds (as we've learned to expect) a summit of inspiration. She's still wearing, loosely, the protective dressing-gown forced on her earlier in the scene. Nearing the point of exit, she shrugs those determined shoulders, stirs those loquacious hips, and the now-disgraced dressing-gown, which slides obediently from her beautiful body, lies pulsing on the floor as the door closes behind her.*

The **Taoiseach** *stands there, battered.*

Soundtrack: far away, far, far away, the ghostly baying of a hound. **Taoiseach** *is now staring at the discarded dressing-gown. He's pulled towards it. He's now standing over it. He gathers it, breath quivering. He looks at it, nostrils heaving. No. He crushes it to a lump, 'decisively' marches to the cupboard, fires it into that dusk. He shuts the cupboard door, locks the cupboard, and stands there.*

Act Two
Scene Five

*Lute chords, milk them. A ray of sunlight (from a small circular window above the main one) picks out the immobilized **Taoiseach**, haloes him. The effect should be to render him incredibly fragile, lost, paradoxically blessed, as the scorched angel is blessed. The sunlight feasts and, as sunlight will, departs. Knock, door opens, enter **Arkins** with tidings.*

Taoiseach Don't tell me he's snuffed it?

Arkins Snuffed it, Taoiseach? He certainly hasn't *snuffed* it.

Taoiseach Continue.

Arkins I'm fresh from the Mauve Room, Taoiseach.

Taoiseach Some shambles that must be. Bring on the fumigators! So. The Inflated-in-Waiting?

Arkins Not that well.

Taoiseach I *know* he's not that well, from his mother dropped him he wasn't *that well*. Can you, you're a poet, aren't you, can you be more precise? I'm glad, by the way, to see you clothed for a change.

Arkins Sorry about that, Taoiseach. Grace was responsible.

Taoiseach I'll warrrant. Mc Phrunty –

Arkins Taoiseach, I was admitted to the Mauve Room as the women took off.

Taoiseach *Took off!* Their great gift! Has it struck you that they're *strippers* out there in the workaday world, that's how they earn their crust!

Arkins Taoiseach –

Taoiseach Continue –

Arkins I kept vigil by the bed, thought about a doctor, he looked very low, then, suddenly, he –

Taoiseach Rose from the dead?

Arkins Touch of that, Taoiseach. His colour came back, he stirred, lifted from the bed –

Taoiseach Mc Phrunty *resurrectus*!

Arkins Lifted from the bed, Taoiseach, muttering he 'must find Grace, must find Grace' –

Taoiseach In Grace salvation! In Elizabeth? Subjugation! *Quelle dominatrix!*

Sheridan *has entered discreetly, bearing a large dinner plate which is covered by an immaculate Kleenex. He rests the place on a convenient table and, dutiful, menial, stands by.*

Arkins Never saw anything like it, Taoiseach. Never will, not if I –

Taoiseach Anything like *what*?

Arkins What overtook him, Taoiseach, just outside the door of the Mauve Room.

Taoiseach Gave birth, did he? Triplets! (*Turning to the audience, giddy*) That's what I love about plays: christenings, weddings, funerals! Yes, Arkins?

Arkins *looks, dramatically, towards the complicit* **Sheridan**, *who fetches the plate from that convenient table, comes forward with it, and, with the lightest hand, removes the discreet Kleenex. In the middle of the plate rests a small pile of ashes.*

Sheridan He self-combusthered, the poor whore.

Arkins (*formal*) Spontaneous combustion, Taoiseach. *Ar dheis Dé agus aráile.*

Taoiseach *is staring at the ashes.*

Taoiseach Wouldn't have thought he had it in him, tell you the truth.

Arkins You're right, Taoiseach. Nothing became him like the leaving. An oval blossom of flame, amethyst mostly, and (*nodding*) behold the remnants.

Sheridan Wicked small left-overs for a big Turk of a man, Taoiseach.

Taoiseach And all this took place – again –

Arkins On the corridor parquet, Taoiseach, just outside the Mauve Room.

Taoiseach (*to* **Sheridan**) Parquet?

Sheridan *Lickeen* of a scorch, Taoiseach, not so you'd notice.

Thunder. Downpour commences. **Taoiseach** *signals* **Sheridan** *to adjust the window. This is done. The* **Taoiseach** *goes, solemnly, to the plate containing the ashes, circles it, observing closely the Layvin's, and, satisfied, moves away.*

Taoiseach He'd drink gin off a specimen abscess, that's what brought it on. With some assistance, fair is fair, from our minges *mirabiles*. Bended knees, please.

Omnes (*kneeling*) Name of the Father, and of the Son, and of the Holy Ghost –

Taoiseach Hail Mary, full of grace, the Lord's is with thee, blessed art thou among women, and blessed is the fruit of thy womb, Jesus.

Arkins/Sheridan Holy Mary, Mother of God, pray for us sinners now and at the hour of our death.

Omnes Name of the Father, and of the Son, and of the Holy Ghost, Amen.

All rise. Storm gathering itself outside. Shower pelting the window.

Taoiseach Sheridan. Safe, please –

Sheridan *to it, moves to the safe, plays with the combination lock, door opens. The* **Taoiseach**, *meanwhile, is, with great care, settling the Kleenex above the ashes.*

Taoiseach *Habeas corpus* – one of the great dictums. DNA does the rest. State Funeral Tuesday. Give him a good send-off.

He stores the plate and contents in the safe and locks it securely.

Taoiseach (*back to business*) Right. Where's my press secretary, anyone know?

Arkins On reconnaisance, I fancy – your guests, Taoiseach.

Taoiseach To be sure. Has the hots. Our Redemptorist turned Casanova!

Wicked downpour hitting stride.

Taoiseach (*exultant*) Sheridan, advise the kitchen, we'll wake poor Mc Phrunty over lunch, hot buttered lobster and half-a-dozen of that chilly-chatty-sting-sting New Zealand white!

Sheridan Certainly, Taoiseach.

Exit **Sheridan**. **Taoiseach** *stares at* **Arkins**, *his vein of exultation is not being shared.*

Taoiseach How can you remain so calm, Arkins? Aren't you asking yourself, 'Where will they stop, these Liliths of a summer morning?' They posit no limits. Everything in swithers and swives, but, know something, Arkins, I find it – what do I find it? – I

find it *galactic* – I find it *lactic* galactic, I find it
pancreatic lactic galactic – and that mix dripping the
incorrigible stink of life! The original loose cannon was
a courtesan – there's a thought for the day! Have they
mounted you yet?

Arkins Taoiseach, you know I'm lavender.

Taoiseach *grabs* **Arkins**, *vehemently sniffs him, throws
him aside.*

Taoiseach Not *that* lavender, you've tupped Bess or
my nose is a brain-dead mallet. What next? They've
had you, Ice-Man Hislop melts to their touch, they've
terminated Mc Phrunty, and I'm running on empty!
5/1 on they've also had Sheridan in the hay! Where are
they, incidentally, where are my beauties?

Is that far thunder we're hearing? A picture of the
Taoiseach *jolts, shifts; it's now hanging crazily. It's
pendulumming.* **Taoiseach** *and* **Arkins** *stare at it, watch
it come to a halt at a wayward angle.* **Arkins** *moves
forward, dutiful, to set it to rights.*

Taoiseach Arkins –

Arkins Taoiseach?

Taoiseach Leave it, leave it, leave it. (*Beat*) 'We order
things and they decay …'

Arkins 'We order them again, and they decay …'

Taoiseach 'We order them again, and we ourselves
decay …'

Arkins Rilke, Taoiseach?

Taoiseach Is it Rilke? Met it in a book somewhere. It stuck. (*Pause*) I don't know what's happening. Does anyone?

Enter **Elizabeth** *and* **Grace**, *lightly clad, summer dresses, and happy.* **Grace** *carries a bunch of daisies. They pay no heed to the men. Mid-stage they halt and embrace voluptuously. Make this a mesmerizing cameo. Over, they make it to exit.*

Taoiseach Ladies?

Grace (*without breaking stride*) Five minutes, *a mhic*. Quickie. Only. Five minutes.

Door opens to them, they're gone. Door closes. The **Taoiseach** *and* **Arkins** *exchange glances.*

Taoiseach They enter dry as snuff from the downpour! Why? Because they *are* the downpour, the sunlight, the daisies, and the dove! They're love on the hoof! Naturally, they lick each other for recreation!

Enter **Hislop**, *naked but for a towel about his waist.* **Hislop** *drenched, mud-stained, and clearly out of it.*

Taoiseach Hislop?

Arkins Are you all right?

Hislop *staggers/is assisted to a chair. They check, slap his cheek, so on. Useless. Eventually, he rouses.*

Hislop (*fury*) Keep away, keep away, keep away –

Taoiseach Are you all right?

Arkins Talk to us, talk to us –

Taoiseach The women? Was it the women?

The word women *seems to jolt* **Hislop** *to clarity. He stands up (violently) and motions the others to stay clear of him.*

Hislop (*déraciné*) Some swim. Don't get wet.

Taoiseach What?

Hislop It's quite simple.

Arkins What do you mean?

Taoiseach It *was* the women, was it?

Hislop (*heedless*) It's quite simple. No questions, please. Some swim, don't get wet. I have to be alone for a while.

Taoiseach Hislop, sit down – we'll get you a –

Hislop *brushes the* **Taoiseach**'s *restraining hands aside.*

Arkins Let him go, let him go, Taoiseach –

Hislop (*to anyone*) And don't get wet.

He walks slowly from the room. A door opens to him. He passes through, door closes.

Taoiseach Will he be all right?

Arkins Let him catch breath – he'll be okay …

Arkins *sits.* **Taoiseach** *tours the space, agitated, hyper. The rain has ceased – sunlight even. It's turned, of a sudden, to a benign summer day. Even a mad supplementary burst of blackbird notes.*

Taoiseach All right.

He sits opposite **Arkins,** *head in hands, briefly looks up.*

Taoiseach Mc Phrunty departed. Hislop – crippled? Who's next?

Arkins I don't know.

Taoiseach Who are they?

Arkins Elizabeth the First and Grace O'Malley – in *succubi* mode.

Taoiseach *Succubi?*

Arkins They move promiscuously between the worlds. Upright, missionary, sixty-nine, marathon, or quickie, infinite variety – as you must surely be aware, Taoiseach – their signature and seal.

Taoiseach Why've they picked me?

Arkins They're choosy.

Taoiseach Grace insists I've been howling for them for at least a decade. Is that possible? Always been taken by them – Grace O'Malley and Elizabeth, who wouldn't? – but *howling* – for at least a decade?

Arkins Taoiseach –

Taoiseach What?

Arkins Few of us know for what we howl. Our fate, some say.

Taoiseach (*not attending*) I have to say – I have to put on record – and I want you to remember this, Arkins, I have never, never ever, experienced anything remotely resembling what they bestow.

Arkins You describe my shared time with them, Taoiseach. Nothing to add to that.

Taoiseach *stands up, looks at the chair on which he's been sitting, kicks the chair savagely. It falls to bits, skidding about the place.* **Taoiseach** *strolls, looking for his next move. He halts.*

Taoiseach What was it you said there – about howling – and fate – what we know, don't know?

Arkins I said, Taoiseach, if I remember correctly – 'Few of us know for what we howl. Our fate, some say …'

Taoiseach Our *fate* – what the hell is that? Your fate. Explain, explain –

Arkins Three goddesses out there, it's in all the stories. One releases you into the world, the next

determines the nature of your life, the third snips the
thread – gone!

Taoiseach Am I stuck with my fate?

Arkins Madness to contest it, it's said.

Taoiseach So it's possible Grace is right – I *may* have
been howling for them for at least a decade?

Arkins Indeed.

Taoiseach They could destroy me!

Arkins That's true. But –

Taoiseach *But?*

Arkins There's really no telling, Taoiseach.

Taoiseach Is that *fair?*

Arkins Not meant to be fair. It, simply, *is.*

Pause.

Taoiseach All right. Your advice?

Arkins Follow your instincts.

Taoiseach They'll be the death of me, Arkins.

Arkins No telling. The obligation is to explore.

Taoiseach (*striding downstage, to audience*) They'll do
for me!

Arkins Repeat: there's no telling. In any case, leaving (*he looks about him*) all this isn't the issue. It's the *nature* of the leaving.

Taoiseach Come again –

Arkins Leaving – earth – isn't the issue. It's the *nature* of the leaving.

Taoiseach You believe that?

Arkins Yes.

Taoiseach You sound like my grandmother. (*Pause*) Don't you want to come with me then – into the merry furnace – or are you the cosy hurler-on-ditch?

Arkins I was about to enquire, Taoiseach –

Taoiseach Yes?

Arkins I'd be more than happy – privileged, may I say – to make it a foursome.

Taoiseach *studies* **Arkins**, *ponders, smiles.*

Taoiseach Full marks, Arkins. You put your money where your cock is – is that a definition of 'following your fate'?

Arkins I've heard worse definitions, Taoiseach.

Taoiseach I'll consider your application, okay? (*He embraces* **Arkins**) Call you for interview! I've always said – 'Have a poet about the place …' I couldn't pay

you for what you've conveyed to me today. (*Pause*) But
– Arkins – this question – what you say about fate –
isn't it all arranged in advance then? Mapped? What
kind of mechanical puppety-puppet is that for a life?
It's all *mapped*?

Arkins Taoiseach –

Taoiseach Sir?

Arkins There's an answer to that question.

Taoiseach Give it to me!

Arkins There's an answer to the question – but it's
not available, they say, until we get to the other side.

Taoiseach We must wait.

Arkins Yes. We must wait.

Taoiseach *sits, gazes out into the audience.* **Arkins** *stands
there, gaze also on the audience.*

Stretch this pause.

*Soundtrack: three well-nigh musical screeches from a
peacock out there somewhere.*

Taoiseach Leave me, Arkins.

ACT TWO
SCENE SIX

A mobile on a table jingles three times. **Taoiseach** *goes, stands over it. It jingles again, three times.*

Taoiseach *walks away from it, wanders.*

Taoiseach (*to house*) Cherie – she sniffs the weather, one of their great gifts ...

It jingles again, three times. **Taoiseach** *to it, engages it.*

Taoiseach Cherie!

From the mobile a blast of unintelligible yappety-yap. **Taoiseach** *moves the mobile back from his ear and audibility declines to eventual silence. Now the* **Taoiseach** *speaks – into the caller's occasional and scarcely audible (to us) contributions.*

Taoiseach *Cherie, je t'aime ... An dtuigeann tú, a chroí? ... Je t'aime ... Toujours ... Sempra, sempra ...Oui, ma belle ... A thaisce, ná bac leis! Oui, oui ... Mais non ... En peu ... Impossible, absolument impossible ... Oui, oui ... Eternellement, Cherie ... Go hiontach! ... Cinnte, cinnte, a thaisce ... Ná bac leis ... A ce soir, a stór, a ce soir ...*

He switches the mobile off, puts it aside, advances morosely to talk to the audience.

Taoiseach Have you ever had the experience of
opening your passport, glancing at your photo, and
discovering that the name under it is Paddy Shite? ...
She's a good woman ...

*He finds a chair, positions it downstage. He will talk
intimately to the audience.*

Taoiseach I don't know how to – I don't know what to
– Arkins goes on about fate – my fate – you mustn't
contest your fate – I've no idea what he's on about – and
yet I do. I do. I do ... Do you take these women to be
your lawful wedded fate? I do. I don't. I'm not sure.
Show (*wildly to the house*) of hands, show of hands,
come on, show of hands! All in favour say *Seá – seá, seá
– SEÁ, SEÁ*! (*The* seá *becomes a manic stutter, prolonged.
He snaps free of it.*) Ceann Comhairle, why don't you
intervene, suspend the sitting – what are you being paid
for? – clear the chamber, declare summer vacation! See
you all in September – when the grapes are purply –
(*singing now*) Margarita picka the grapes with me!

He's now on his feet, moving about, distrait, *visibly. He
takes a grip on himself.*

Taoiseach Excuse the outburst. I will not impose.
There's a door here. Somewhere. I think I see a door.
Somewhere. Nearby. A white door ...

*He looks about him, sees the chair he has kicked asunder.
He wanders to it, picks it up, tries vaguely to put it
together again, but fails. He throws it aside.*

Taoiseach (*to chair wreckage*) I'd burn you on the spot
if it weren't for the Corpo Fire-Regulations. (*Stops dead,*

adrift) Fused, fused, fused the two of them even more
beautiful.

*He wanders to a door, stands with his back to it, takes out
a hanky. He seems to be on automatic pilot, and
commences polishing the doorknob. He gives up on that,
delivers himself to the audience again.*

Taoiseach   I can go *this* far with Arkins. If fate – *FATE*
– is being pulled irresistibly towards a line of action, then
this is – *they are* – my fate. And if you say to me, have
you been walking towards them from the cradle, I'd have
to say yes. YES. *YES*. Why? Because of what they *do* to
me. What's that? It's where I've never been before. In bed.
Or outa bed. It's – it's – don't ask me what it is. (*Pause*)
There's only one catch. Death. Rot. Quite. Possibly. The
box. The graveyard speeches. I want *that*? Then Arkins
says – 'No tellin', no tellin', and, anyway, *the readiness is
all*,' and wants in on the romp! I like him – but no, no.
Selfish to the last! (*Long pause*) My feet are frozen. (*Looks
at his feet*) Cold feet isn't just a phrase, you know that?
Fear – know what that is, *F-E-A-R*, it lowers the blood
temperature. Starting with the feet. Then works up.
Finally – what? You're a block of ice. A *stalactite*, it's
called. The contrary of departure by spontaneous
combustion. God be with Mc Phrunty. Who'd have
forecast that for *him*?

A knock on the door. Enter **Arkins**, *who stands there,
seeking permission to enter, to participate. The* **Taoiseach**
views him, shakes his head. **Arkins** *leaves.*

Taoiseach   Any gamblers among you? I keep a few
race-horses. The father a close friend of Morny Wing,

the great jockey. Mornington Wing – what a name for a
jockey! Had I been named Mornington Wing I'd have
been fine. Or if I'd had a child – girl-child – called
Morning. A girl-child called Morning – whom I could
have watched playing. Or picking primroses in March.
Or staring, astonished, at a white horse. (*Long pause*)
Tell you something, and for free: I'm minded to gamble
– just go for it – y'know, like closin' your eyes and
walking over a cliff. Donegal. Or Clare. Aran Islands.
Am I going mad? I feel in balance. I think. (*Again a
burst of the cacaphonic* seá, seá, seá, seá. *He recovers*) I
want the trip. Am I ready to pay the price? Will there
be a price? Always a price. For coming. Going. Pray for
me. Pray for Grace. Pray for Liz. Pray for us all. Amen.

He presses the buzzer for **Sheridan**. **Sheridan** *appears.*

Sheridan Taoiseach?

Taoiseach Summon the household, would you,
Sheridan –

Sheridan To be sure, Taoiseach. *Household*, Taoiseach?

Taoiseach That's what I said.

Sheridan Would that include, Taoiseach –

Taoiseach My guests? They are not of the household.
Of my destiny, more like it. A larger issue. I want you,
my wife, and Arkins and Hislop – as honorary
members of the intimate household – here assembled.

Sheridan Done, Taoiseach.

Exit **Sheridan**.

Taoiseach Now you're thinking – 'Grandstanding to the last!' Perhaps. Yet it seems appropriate – for this hour – the cliff-top, roar of the waves, pull of the sea … Mornington Wing – what a name for a jockey! He died young, by the way, relatively young. A chill. Gone. I believe – but I may be composing as I go along – at any rate, I believe I once met a child called Morning – she was gathering primroses, bright green morning … White horse watching her from an adjoining field …

Enter the **Wife, Arkins, Hislop, Sheridan.** *They sit here and there. The* **Taoiseach** *approaches, views them calmly.*

Taoiseach Thank you for coming. At this hour. I wanted to say a few words. Now that you're here, that's not my inclination at all. Sometimes I think I've been cursed with words. Shouting is not the vice of the Celt, as alleged. Talking, rather. We just can't shut up.

He goes to the **Wife,** *takes her by the hand, leads her aside. He examines her palms, musingly, as soothsayer might.*

Taoiseach Such soft fingers … (*He kisses her affectionately*) *Tóg bog é.*

Wife Who are you?

Taoiseach I don't know.

Wife *exits slowly.* **Taoiseach** *studies those remaining. Signals to* **Arkins.** **Arkins** *presents himself.*

Taoiseach Give me your definition of a poet again?

Arkins 'Death to love a poet, death to marry a poet, death to be a poet!'

Taoiseach Arkins, I want you to do one other thing for me.

Arkins Taoiseach?

Taoiseach Once a year, at least, the wine flowing, you ask us all to fall in love with the word for *sea* in a certain European language.

Arkins *nods agreement.*

Taoiseach May I hear again from your lips, Arkins, the Greek word for *sea*?

Arkins *Thalassa* ...

Taoiseach Say it several times, please –

Arkins *Thalassa, thalassa, thalassa* ...

Taoiseach *Thalassa* ...

Taoiseach *hugs* **Arkins**. *Exit* **Arkins**.

Taoiseach *Fairrge* isn't bad either ... *Fairrge* ... And *sea* is an audible movement, isn't it – *sea*, the say, o, the say ...

Hislop, *still in a state, rises and leaves the space.*
Taoiseach *waves him off affectionately and nods to*
Sheridan. Sheridan *joins him.* **Taoiseach** *hugs him, a laugh and deep camaraderie in the hug.*

Taoiseach   Question, Sheridan –

Sheridan   Taoiseach?

Taoiseach   What did you do when you realised you'd thumbed the hearse?

Sheridan   Skipped over the ditch, Taoiseach!

Taoiseach   The best of your play. Take care of her, will you?

Sheridan   To be sure, Taoiseach.

Easy farewell hug. Exit **Sheridan**.

Enter **Grace** *and* **Elizabeth**. *They're dressed as when we first met them. And they exude showdown.*

Taoiseach *greets them calmly.*

Taoiseach   Do sit down, Ladies.

The two sit. **Taoiseach** *to the safe, opens it, brings the plate to them, dramatically removes the Kleenex.*

Taoiseach   You've heard?

Grace   Sheridan told us, yes.

The two inspect. **Grace** *sniffs the layvin's.*

Grace   That's him all right.

Elizabeth   The flowering of Mc Phrunty!

Grace (*wrappy-uppy*) God be with the poor divil.

Taoiseach, *serene, returns the ashes to the safe. He sits.*

Taoiseach A word, if I may –

They wave him on.

Taoiseach Basically, I'm in agreement. Ten years is enough of waiting.

Grace He's ripe, God bless him, on the bough!

Taoiseach I begin to understand why you're here. I think we should meet the moment, let it take us where it will.

Elizabeth He understands –

Grace Doesn't have to be understood!

Taoiseach Only one thing – I have one question – if I may –

Grace Yes?

Taoiseach Does our – adventure – of necessity – have to involve –

Taoiseach *stops, the two women never more in charge.*

Taoiseach It's all right. No questions.

Grace You're sure?

Elizabeth Ask it.

Grace We don't bite!

Elizabeth We consume!

Taoiseach You've answered me.

Grace We have?

Taoiseach Just by being, yes. Let's go for it.

Grace And damn'd be him – or her –

Elizabeth Who cries – 'Hold enough!'

The atmosphere changes utterly. All stand. **Elizabeth** *takes from her bosom a blood-red apple, studies it, kisses it, takes a large bite, slings it to* **Grace**. **Grace** *studies it, licks it lovingly, takes a large bite, slings it to the* **Taoiseach**. **Taoiseach** *studies it, holds it aloft as you'd raise a glass of wine. Deep breath, he takes a large bite, throws the remains over his left shoulder.*

Pause.

Joining **Elizabeth**, **Grace** *produces from her bosom a snake three or four times (on the basis of what we can see) the size of the previous snake* (Scene Four).

'Activating the object' (as they say in the theatre), the two embrace and, the snake writhing companionably about them, they stroll from the room, door opening to their advance and remaining open.

The **Taoiseach** *has witnessed, as in* witnessed, *all this. Now he looks, sombre, at that open door. He's not ready* *yet, it seems. His gaze leaves the open door. He finds a place to sit. He sits, looks at, and through, the audience. Just when you've decided he's going to be there forever, he rises and walks slowly through that open door. Slow fade. A modest spot contests the slow fade. Finally, this spot is vivid and focused trimly on what's left of that apple. It brushes that apple.*

Black-out.

End.